Torah means teaching or instruction.
The 10 Commandments are our wedding vows,
the marriage Covenant we'll celebrate at the Marriage Supper.
Yisharal (Israel) is Yahuah's wife, and all who join to Yahuah do
so through the same Covenant. There is one Torah for all.
Wormwood is expressed as a bitterness toward Yahuah's Word
and Name, and the evidence is the disuse of them.
The dragon wants to remove and alter Yahuah's Word
as was done in the garden of Eden.
WITHOUT THE COVENANT, WE ARE LAWLESS

WORMWOOD
THE GOSPEL OF LAWLESSNESS
The Cause: A Bitterness Toward Obedience

If the Torah (called the law by pastors) was done away with after
Yahusha died and resurrected, then why is the dragon
to fight with those guarding it?

"**And the dragon was enraged with the ashah** (woman), **and he went to fight with the remnant of her seed, those guarding the Commands of Yahuah and possessing the witness of Yahusha haMashiak.**" Revelation 12:17

While claiming obedience unnecessary, they demand the tithe.
For You Have Made Great Your Word,
Your Name, Above All (From Psalm 138:2)

From the Series: ***Strongholds & False Beliefs***
Doctrines of the World Order, the reign of Babel
Nimrod's World Order will vanish like a vapor, and the eternal
reign of **Yahusha** will come suddenly. His envoys are here.
The **religion of traditions** will be burnt to the ground in one day.
None of men's traditions will survive the Second Coming.

Printed book ISBN: 9781532310409

Lew White - Teacher of Theological Archaeology
Author's research spans 1983 to 2016
Copyright © 2016 by Lew White
Published by Torah Institute
POB 436044, Louisville, KY 40253 USA
502-261-9833
For more information visit
fossilizedcustoms.com - torahzone.net - amazon.com
TORAH INSTITUTE'S YOUTUBE CHANNEL
Visit Facebook: Lew White, BYNV, & Torah Institute
TORAH INSTITUTE, POB 436044, LOUISVILLE, KY 40253-6044
ORDERING BY PHONE: 502-261-9833

"O, What a tangled web we weave, when first we practice to deceive."
Walter Scott

CONTENTS

FEEDING ON WORMWOOD

We are all born into a world of great darkness, as if behind enemy lines.
We are brain-washed from birth to accept the Worldly Order as it is.
**Asherah trees, wreaths, eggs, bunnies, cakes, candles - although
witchcraft, the worldly mind only sees it all as beautiful.**

Abiding in Yahuah's Word sets us free from false beliefs.
Changing Yahuah's Word causes another effect:
They will feed on WORMWOOD, the secret of lawlessness.

This book reveals how a root of bitterness toward obeying
Yahuah's Word grew up in the early forms of Christianity, and
how they persecuted the Natsarim they encountered who kept
the Commandments. Keeping Commandments was considered
heresy to the church fathers, and doctrines developed based on
the patterns of Sun worship.
The Roman Timeline of dogmas and bulls reflects a close
similarity with Hinduism, and now the Information Age is causing
an awakening.
You will see the distinction between one who serves Yahuah,
and one who does not serve Him. This book may be a great
starting point for sharing the naked Truth with those who are fast
asleep in the dream world of religion. The Alexandrian church
fathers disassociated themselves from all behavior resembling
what we see in Scripture. Anyone who observed Torah or used
terminology reflecting similarities with the Yahudim was taxed by
the Fiscus Judaicus, and the revenue was sent to support the
Sun worshipping magisterium of Rome.
The final blow to wormwood is the revealing of who Easter is.
When Christians learn that Easter is Ishtar, the Harlot of Babel,
they will see they were in the Mother of Harlots. This awakening
will break the spell of wormwood, and the bitterness toward
obedience will vaporize.

THE FIRST WORMWOOD
**When the serpent changed the Words of Yahuah,
the first woman was deceived by them.
All mankind is fallen because of wormwood and pretending
the Living Words have been changed.
She ate the wormwood, and it happened in a perfect garden.
Our restoration begins by restoring the Living Words.**

THE BEAST HAD AN ARCHITECT

The **Great Architect** of Sun worship was Nimrod, and was deified by the Babylonians. The beast's hierarchy continues to honor Nimrod as the Sun in symbolic ways using obelisks, crosses, haloes, as well as terminology and maxims.
The beast is the reign of Babel. Yahusha's reign will replace it. Nimrod is the lawless antithesis of the Mashiak. Whose image and inscription is on our currency of exchange? **"IN GOD WE TRUST"** takes on a strange meaning when you look up the origin of the word GOD. Let's examine the word's origin:

WHO IS GOD THEY REFER TO?

GOD (god): **"Common Teutonic word for personal object of religious worship, FORMERLY APPLICABLE TO SUPER-HUMAN BEINGS OF HEATHEN MYTH; on conversion of Teutonic races to Christianity, TERM WAS APPLIED TO SUPREME BEING."** (Encyclopedia Americana, 1945)

Super-human beings are mentioned in this worldly resource. Nimrod, the mighty hunter *who became a mighty one*, was a real man who developed into a heathen myth, literally a sun deity. This is verification that a fallen creature is deceiving the whole world, and has successfully hood-winked the nations to conform to a pattern he instituted long ago in Babylon under **Nimrod**. Alexander Hislop connected the dots (over 100 years ago) that the papacy was disguised Nimrod worship. The beast began with Nimrod, the Great Architect of the Worldly Order, and the tower of Babel. The reign of Babel will continue until Yahusha returns and takes it completely out of the way forever. When your eyes are opened to the Truth, you'll see the Nimrod influence everywhere.
The Freemasons know they worship "Lucifer," the light-bringer. They knowingly revere Nimrod as the Great Architect.
Paul told Timothy people would turn aside to MYTHS, shunning sound doctrine.
"In the presence of Alahim and of Mashiak Yahusha,
Who will judge the living and the dead, and in view of His
appearing and His Reign, I give you this charge:
Preach the Word; be prepared in season and out of season;
correct, rebuke and encourage-with great patience and

careful instruction. For the time will come when men will not put up with sound doctrine. Instead, to suit their own desires, they will gather around them a great number of teachers to say what their itching ears want to hear. They will turn their ears away from the truth and turn aside to myths. But you, keep your head in all situations, endure hardship, do the work of an evangelist, discharge all the duties of your ministry." - 2 Tim 4:1-5

A STAR NAMED WORMWOOD

"And the 3rd messenger sounded, and a great star fell from the heaven, burning like a torch, and it fell on a 3rd of the rivers and on the fountains of water, and the name of the star is called Wormwood. And a 3rd of the waters became wormwood, and many men died from the waters, because they were made bitter." - Rev 8:10,11

PHYSICAL WORMWOOD - MORTAL BITTERNESS
This can be asteroids, war, poison, disease, floods, earthquakes, radiation, crime, and all other fruits of lawlessness.
SPIRITUAL WORMWOOD - BITTERNESS TOWARD TORAH
This is seen in the behavior of people, and is the result of ignoring or altering the Instructions (Torah) of Yahuah.
It's like a programming flaw, or a computer virus, that corrupts from the inside. They feel bitter toward obeying.
The origin of this wormwood is the spiritual realm, where our enemy works through people, corrupting their hearts with **strongholds** (faulty thinking). They feel hatred for the Word.

YAHUAH CALLS ALTERED TEACHINGS "WORMWOOD"
Amus 5:7: **"O you who are turning right-ruling to wormwood, and have cast down righteousness to the Earth!"**

This describes the **alteration** of His Words, by *false teachers*:
Jer/YirmeYahu 9:13-16: **"And Yahuah says, 'Because they have forsaken My Torah which I set before them, and have not obeyed My voice, nor walked according to it, but they have walked according to the stubbornness of their own heart and after the Baalim** (LORDS) **which their fathers had taught them.' Therefore thus said Yahuah Tsabaoth, the Alahim of Yisharal:**

6

'See, I am making this people eat wormwood, and I shall make them drink poisoned water. And I shall scatter them among the gentiles, whom neither they nor their fathers have known. And I shall send a sword after them until I have consumed them.'"

LITERAL & FIGURATIVE WORMWOOD

Misinterpretations can corrupt our understanding, and impact our behavior. Consider Psalms/Tehillim 1:3:

"He is like a *tree* planted by *streams of water*, which yields its *fruit* in season, and whose *leaf* does not *wither"*.

By confusing idiomatic abstractions to be literal, we mistake what Yahuah means. Yahuah expresses His thoughts **abstractly** with metaphors and idioms. Hebrew contains hundreds of idioms.

A person who meditates on the **Torah of Yahuah** is <u>*like*</u> certain things; other elements are symbolic:

Tree: *upright, righteous one*
Streams of water: *Words of Torah*
Fruit: *good character, behavior*
Unwithered leaf: *prosperity*

There is nothing mystical about Yahuah's ideas, but His thoughts **are** higher than ours. All He expects of us is to submit to Him, and trust Him – but there is another who wants to be like Him. That being is an interloper and imposter. A demonic stronghold is like a computer virus corrupting an operating system: our reasoning is misled by faulty information. We need to crash-dump and start over with Truth.

We have to **reprogram our thinking** by **renewing our minds:**

"Oh, the depth of riches, and wisdom and knowledge of Alahim! How unsearchable His judgments and untraceable His ways! For who has known *the mind* of Yahuah? Or who has become His counsellor? Or who first gave to Him, and it shall be given back to him? Because of Him, and through Him, and to Him, are all, to whom be esteem forever, Amn. I call upon you, therefore, brothers, through the compassion of Alahim, to *present your bodies* a living offering – set-apart, well-pleasing to Alahim – your reasonable worship. And do not be conformed to this world, but be transformed by the *renewing of your mind*, so that you prove what is that good and well-pleasing and perfect desire of Alahim."

– Romans 11:33 – 12:2

FROM WORMWOOD
WE LEARN
TO DO THINGS

YAHUAH TOLD US TO NEVER DO

FALLEN DOWN DRUNK

Revelation 2 shows us the *teachings* of Izebel have corrupted the assembly.

She is the church, aka KIRKE, witchery causing drunkenness through false teachings held in a golden cup, Babel. (this same woman is mentioned at Rev 18, but called the mother of harlots) ***"To the Torah and to the witness; If they do not speak according to this Word, it is because they have no daybreak."*** Is. / YashaYahu 8:20

The terms bride, first-fruits, lake of fire, beast, false prophet, living water, bosom of Abraham, green tree, dry tree, eye of a needle, evil eye, and so on are ***idioms***, which is why they are misunderstood and always have been by the Alexandrian Culture (circus fathers). Izebel was a real person, but at Rev. 2 her **teachings** are what Yahusha has against the assembly. Izebel, a witch, taught the 10 northern tribes the fertility behavior - and the **Christmas tree** is one of the remnants. The **yule** (Celtic word for feast) at the time of the solstice, the adoption of heathen **symbols** of fertility, and the shunning of all Yahuah commanded for us to do (i.e., the **rest** on the 7th day as Hebrews 4 calls it) is the result of wormwood corrupting our hearts. By neglecting Shabath, Passover, Unleavened Bread, First-Fruits, Shabuoth, Yom Teruah, Yom Kafar, and Sukkoth we are left with no sign that we serve Yahuah. Resting on Shabath is **the sign forever** between Yahuah and His people. If we are

His people, we have this mark on us; if not, we aren't His. Shabath is called the sign of the *everlasting Covenant.* (see Ez 20:20, Ex 31:16) Instead of Shabath and the festivals Yahusha lived by, Christianity inherited the **Day of the Sun**, enforced by the council of Laodicea (circa 365 CE).

This council outlawed resting on the 7th day under penalty of death. Shabath is the day Yahuah blessed, and the day Yahusha said He was the Master of. This day was edited out of the Living Words, and those who did it claim the apostles did it because Yahusha rose from the dead on the first day of the week.

No one can find the evidence of this of course, but it is believed because it is repeated over and over.

This **alteration** of the Word of Yahuah (Dan. 7:25) is what He calls **wormwood** (Amus 5:7) - and changing His Words is how witchcraft (rebellion) has become institutionalized.

In 1985 I asked my Christian pastor if it was alright with him if I rested on the 7th day of each week, as **"it is written."** He said I'd be **Judaizing** if I did. Commandment-keepers don't fit into the Christian mindset. There's no sin for guarding the Commandments. If you observe the correct day, they condemn you as they chew on a ham sandwich (see YashaYahu 66:17).

The nations have inherited ONLY falsehood, futility, and there is no value in them (YirmeYahu / Jer. 16:19).

There's no mention in Scripture that resting on the 7th day is any kind of offense at all, but it offends the **teaching authority** of men. Natsarim (Acts 24:5, YirmeYahu 31:6) have always rejected the **teaching authority** of men, and choose instead to obey Yahuah. The *first-fruits* (bride, Natsarim) obey the Commandments of Yahuah, and hold to the testimony of Yahusha (Rev. 12 & 14).

Bringing a detestable thing into our homes (a tree) makes us accursed like it (Dt. 7).

The **decorated tree** is an occult object of fertility (phallus, testicles, semen), as is the **wreath** (vagina).

This is rebellion (witchcraft) from the **teaching authority** of Izebel (Rev. 2). Wormwood leads to madness.

DEFINITION OF PSYCHOSIS:

Psychosis is a loss of contact with **reality** that usually includes: *False beliefs* about what is taking place or who one is; seeing or hearing things that *aren't there* (hallucinations).

A person's thinking is corrupted when they follow men's teaching authority, and shun the Torah of Yahuah. If they do not speak according to Torah, they have no light. If they turn their ears **away** from hearing Torah, even their prayer is an abomination. (YashaYahu 8:20, Proverbs 28:9)

WHO'S WHO? Proverbs 28:4:
"Those who forsake the Torah praise the wrong, Those who guard the Torah strive with them."

Read that again slowly, and let's do a little test right now.

Wormwood Test:
Who is serving the dragon, and who is serving Yahusha?
Test yourself with the evidence. Wormwood is feeding on, and living by, alterations of Yahuah's Words.

Pastors and their followers keep repeating they are not "under the law" and don't live by the "old law" because the Commandments were "fulfilled by Yahusha <u>for</u> us" and obedience is no longer required for our deliverance. They say the Torah was a curse, and we are no longer "under the law." People who obey are legalists.
    (aka: heretics, living according to a "false gospel")

If that is the case, then why does the **dragon "make war with a remnant"** who **"keep the Commandments of Yahuah"** and **acknowledge Yahusha** – seen at Revelation 12:17?
Who does that make those who are making war on the Hebrew Roots and the Natsarim who teach obedience?
"And the dragon was enraged with the woman, and he went to fight with the remnant of her seed, those guarding the Commands of Alahim and possessing the witness of Yahusha ha Mashiak." – Rev 12:17

Were you unknowingly taught to practice witchcraft?
Most people are beguiled by traditions, and have very little contact with the Words of Scripture. Using Scripture to evaluate our behavior shows us how witchcraft (rebellion) is employed in unsuspecting ways. Wormwood (bitterness toward Yahuah and His Torah) results in witchcraft (active rebellion against His Word).

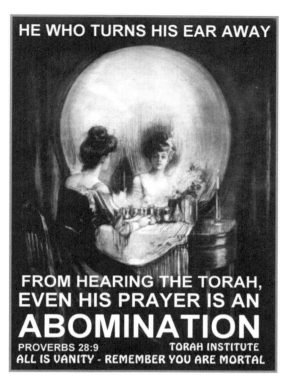

HE WHO TURNS HIS EAR AWAY

FROM HEARING THE TORAH, EVEN HIS PRAYER IS AN **ABOMINATION**

PROVERBS 28:9   TORAH INSTITUTE

ALL IS VANITY - REMEMBER YOU ARE MORTAL

Art: All Is Vanity - Adapted from Charles Allan Gilbert (Lived 1873 – 1929)

Pastors are increasingly asking one another in their own words, **"What is the true Gospel?"** We need to learn how the Torah Yahusha taught is the core of the message of deliverance based on how He answered the young man who asked Him how he might gain eternal life (Mt. 19:16):

He answered the young man, **"Guard the Commandments."** Most people follow a "Gospel of Lawlessness" because they are fed wormwood, a bitterness toward the idea of submitting to the Torah's easy instruction in how to love. They get this from men, not the Word of Yahuah.

THE TORAH IS A MIRROR

"And become doers of the Word, and not hearers only, deceiving yourselves. Because if anyone is a hearer of the Word and not a doer, he is like a man who looks at his natural face in a mirror, for he looks at himself, and goes away, and immediately forgets what he was like. But he that looked into the perfect Torah, that of freedom, and continues in it, not becoming a hearer that forgets, but a

doer of work, this one shall be blessed in his doing of the Torah." - YaAqob / James 1:22-25

BITTERNESS BRINGS DEATH
"And the 3rd messenger sounded, and a great star fell from the heaven, burning like a torch, and it fell on a third of the rivers and on the fountains of water, and the name of the star is called Wormwood. And a 3rd of the mayim became wormwood, and many men died." - Revelation 8:10-11

OBEYING WOULD HAVE BEEN EASIER
"And Yahuah says, 'Because they have forsaken My Turah which I set before them, and have not obeyed My voice, nor walked according to it, but they have walked according to the stubbornness of their own heart and after the Baalim, which their fathers had taught them.' Therefore thus said Yahuah Tsabaoth, the Alahim of Yisharal, 'See, I am making this people eat wormwood, and I shall make them drink poisoned water. And I shall scatter them among the gentiles, whom neither they nor their fathers have known. And I shall send a sword after them until I have consumed them.'" - YirmeYahu / Jeremiah 9:13-16

Sins are crimes against love. Sins stay in the echo-chamber (the world) and their effects cascade into others' lives all around us. The training in love we receive from the Ten Commandments gives us the wisdom to reflect the character of Yahuah in all we say and do. We possess the power to stop all crime by simply teaching and obeying the Living Words. They produce the fruits of the Spirit: love, joy, peace, patience, kindness, goodness, gentleness, faithfulness, and self-control. (Galatians 5)

Belief alone, without perfecting it by our actions, is dead belief. Love one another as Yahusha loves you. If everyone practiced what the Living Words tell us to do from the mouth of Yahuah for a single day, there would be nothing evil to report in the media. It would be **"The Day The Earth Stood Still."**

THE AMBASSADORS HAVE ARRIVED
Just for the sake of argument, why would this book refer to so many Scriptures to prompt you to obey, if it served the objectives of the dragon? On the other hand, those teaching us to disobey use twisted interpretations to accomplish their goal.

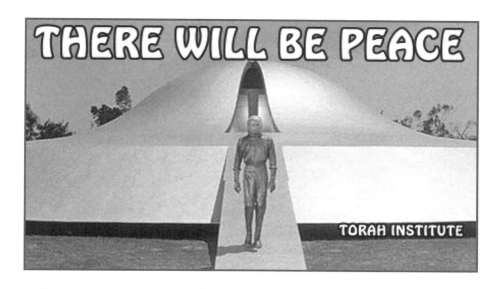

THERE WILL BE PEACE

TORAH INSTITUTE

Nations have been annihilating one another since the time of Nimrod, and even before the flood there was continual violence, as well as genetic corruption by the fallen ones (Nephilim).
When I was a child I loved the 1951 movie called ***The Day The Earth Stood Still***. There is a decision everyone must make.
A ship from outside this world lands in a baseball field in Washington D.C. to bring the inhabitants of Earth a message they could not ignore. The being on board was an **envoy** named **Klaatu**, and he came to tell all the nations of Earth they must learn to live peacefully, or suffer **utter annihilation.** Earth was reaching the point of becoming a threat to other inhabited worlds, and so one robotic policeman (Gort) was used to prove how powerful the alien civilization was. The movie captures the essence of the final warning we find at Malaki 4:1-6:
"'For look, the yom shall come, burning like a furnace, and all the proud, and every wrongdoer shall be stubble. And the yom that shall come shall burn them up,' said Yahuah Tsabaoth, 'which leaves to them neither root nor branch. But to you who fear My Name the Servant of Uprightness shall arise with healing in His wings. And you shall go out and leap for joy like calves from the stall. And you shall trample the wrongdoers, for they shall be ashes under the soles of your feet on the yom that I do this,' said Yahuah Tsabaoth. 'Remember the Turah of Mosheh, My servant, which I commanded him in Koreb for all Yisharal – laws and

right-rulings. See, I am sending you Aliyah the Prophet before the coming of the great and awesome yom of Yahuah. And he shall turn the hearts of the fathers to the children, and the hearts of the children to their fathers, lest I come and smite the arets with utter destruction.'"
– Malaki 4:1-6 BYNV

The warning to get in line or else is a strong correlation with the plot of the movie, *The Day The Earth Stood Still*. How to prepare for the end is explained here very clearly. Note that the preparation for the Return of Yahusha at the time of the "**Day of Yahuah**" is preceded by the **warning** to remember the Turah of Mosheh. Specifically, this is the 10 Commandments. When these are obeyed and lived by Yahusha's Natsarim, we are accused of being "legalists," as if "legalism" (lawfulness) is a bad thing.
Good is called evil, and evil is called good.
Everyone should strive to be legal, not illegal.
We have to listen to the warning and enjoin to the Covenant of love, obeying the Ten Commandments.
Our thinking became off-course about what is expected of us.
It's as if someone rewired our alarm system so we won't know when our behavior is offensive to Yahuah.

NATSARIM: ENVOYS BEARING A MESSAGE
"**Therefore we are envoys on behalf of Mashiak, as though Alahim were pleading through us. We beg, on behalf of Mashiak: Be restored to favor with Alahim.**"– 2 Korinthians 5:20

THE LAWLESSNESS ONE WILL BE REVEALED

"And now you know what restrains, for him to be revealed in his time. For the secret of lawlessness is already at work – only until he who now restrains comes out of the midst. And then the lawless one shall be revealed, whom the Master shall consume with the Spirit of His mouth and bring to naught with the manifestation of His coming.

The coming of the *lawless one* is according to the working of satan, with all power and signs and wonders of falsehood, and with all deceit of unrighteousness in those perishing, because they did not receive the love of the Truth in order for them to be saved.

And for this reason Alahim sends them a working of delusion for them to believe the falsehood, in order that all should be judged who did not believe the Truth, but have delighted in the unrighteousness." – 2 Thess. 2:6-12

The prophet Isaiah / YashaYahu tells us precisely why Yahuah will burn the Earth on the Day of Yahuah. Our teachers are the cause for hardly anyone knowing why:

24:3-6: "The erets is completely emptied and utterly plundered, for Yahuah has spoken this word.

The arets shall mourn and wither, the world shall languish and wither, the haughty people of the arets shall languish.

For the arets has been defiled under its inhabitants, because they have transgressed the Toroth*, changed the law, broken the Everlasting Covenant.

Therefore a curse shall consume the arets, and those who dwell in it be punished. Therefore the inhabitants of the arets shall be burned, and few men shall be left."

- YashaYahu / Isaiah 24:3-6 ***Toroth** - plural of Torah, instruction.

WORMWOOD IS A CHANGED MESSAGE

"But the message of Yahuah you no longer remember! For every man's message is his own word, for you have changed the Words of the living Alahim, Yahuah of Tsabaoth, our Alahim!" – YirmeYahu / Jeremiah 23:36

The teachers fail to tell us the Covenant is "everlasting," but insist it has been "done away" and "nailed to the crux."

If it was annulled, why then would there be a **remnant** obeying the **Commandments of Yahuah in the last days**, and being pursued by the dragon? **Whose side are we on?** (see Rev. 12) The Alexandrian fathers have lied to us. Their teachings have passed-down to all the pastors receiving tithes to spread their message (gospel) of lawlessness:

WORMWOOD, a bitter attitude toward Torah.

This is the only reason, according to all Scriptures, why the whole Earth shall be burned in the day of judgment – see also 13:9, 13:11, 26:21, 66:24, Mic. 5:15, Zeph. 1:2-18.

WORMWOOD – LIKE SEEDLESS FRUIT (GMO)

Man does not live by bread alone, but by every Word that proceeds from the mouth of Yahuah.

What if His Word is altered, and the seed is no longer in that which grows up because men changed it? It then becomes like genetically-modified food. It looks the same on the outside, but it does not contain LIFE inside itself.

Living foods can reproduce, but not GMO's.

Two Views Of Galatians

"You observe days and months and seasons and years" - Gal 4:10 The Galatians were formerly pagans and observing the days they were conditioned to from their youth. Paul refers to the flesh and Spirit (Hagar and Sarah) to give support to obedience, not to dismiss Torah.

Gal 4:29: "But, as he who was born according to the flesh then persecuted him born according to the Spirit, so also now." We who obey are persecuted by the lawless because we walk in the power of Yahusha's Spirit, having received a love for the Truth.

16

The mindset of the lawless is formed by altering Yahuah's Words, what He calls eating "**wormwood**." We who obey Torah strive with them to wake up and detox their minds from men's teachings that keep them asleep, as though they are drugged. Yahuah did not change His Commandments, but He sent us His Paraklita (Yahusha's Spirit of Truth to live in us) to give us His view of the world. We can love Yahuah and one another (the fruit of obedience) by the implanted Word. The birds have stolen the Seed (the Commandments) from those who do not have ears to hear their Master's Voice.

Those bound by Christian teachings feel that the days, months, seasons, and years Paul refers to are those that Yahusha Himself lived by, which we are to walk in also. The logical flaw most miss is that the Galatians had never been conditioned to follow the Way of Truth because they were converts, so they would not be "reverting back" to any other pattern but their original pagan ways they had vomited-up at the time they converted.

A person raised in the mindset that the Sabbaths and festivals of Yahuah were like Rahab (fleshly) has been eating wormwood (altered teachings). Paul was very pro-Torah, but exposed the yoke of men's teachings (Yahudaism, his former way). Paul refers to his former way in Yahudaism to be the "teachings of the fathers" - the rabbi's - but never the yoke of Torah.

Yahusha also directly confronted the rabbinical way for having set aside the Commandments of Yahuah in order to keep their own traditions, which were the commandments of men.

THE GREATEST QUESTION EVER ASKED (Mt. 19:16-19):
"Now a man came up to Yahusha and asked,
'Rabbi, what good thing must I do to attain eternal life?'
'Why do you ask me about what is good?' **Yahusha replied.**
'There is only One Who is good.
If you want to enter life, obey the Commandments.'
'Which ones?' **the man inquired. Yahusha replied,**
'You do not murder, you do not commit adultery, you do not steal, you do not give false testimony, you honor your father and mother,' **and** *'love your neighbor as yourself.'"*

He was referring to Ex. 20, Deut. 5, Lev. 19.
All Scripture is *Yahuah-breathed*, 2 Timothy 3:16, 17 (BYNV):

"All Writing *[graphe]* is breathed by Yahuah and profitable for teaching, for reproof, for setting straight, for instruction in uprightness, that the man of Yahuah might be fitted, equipped for every good work."

The Torah **_defines_** what is sin (1 John 3:4) - but if we are programmed to disobey for whatever reason, thinking what was a sin is no longer a sin because of our "liberty" from the Commandments, we have come under the influence of a serious delusion, and our "seared" conscience will not warn us of the problem.
Our liberty is from SIN, not law.

PAUL IS MISUNDERSTOOD
Paul did not intend to say we are to disobey Torah, but the Torah we are not under is the penalty prescribed by Torah (death). Yahusha's blood redeems us from the penalty of our crimes. He didn't die to take away the definition of sin.
He redeemed us from sin - not to sin.
www.fossilizedcustoms.com/cheirographon.html

TRIBULATION TIMES WILL WAKE THEM UP
YirmeYahu / Jeremiah16:16-19:
"'See, I am sending for many fishermen,' declares Yahuah, 'and they shall fish them. And after that I shall send for many hunters, and they shall hunt them from every mountain and every hill, and out of the holes of the rocks. For My eyes are on all their ways; they have not been hidden from My face, nor has their crookedness been hidden from My eyes.
And first I shall repay double for their crookedness and their sin, because they have defiled My land with the dead bodies of their disgusting *matters*, and have filled My inheritance with their abominations.'
O Yahuah, my strength and my stronghold and my refuge, in the day of distress the gentiles shall come to You from the ends of the earth and say, 'Our fathers have inherited only falsehood, futility, and there is no value in them.'"
The lawless (wicked) will not understand, but in the last days there is to be a purification process:

"Many will be purified, made spotless and refined, but the wicked will continue to be wicked. None of the wicked will understand, but those who are wise will understand." – Danial 12:10

Our obedience isn't what delivers us, but it is evidence of our faith, and evidence that we are being saved. We obey because we are delivered. Our wills are controlled by the TORAH, the "Living Word" (Heb. 4) -- which is the mind of the Spirit of Yahusha.

Acts 5:32 says that the Spirit (of Yahusha) is only given to those who *obey* Him. This is "receiving a love for the TRUTH," and since His WORD, the TORAH, is what TRUTH is, receiving a love for it changes our personality, and the result is we walk in the mind of Yahusha's Spirit, enabled to love the Commandments. Receiving the Mind of the Spirit of Yahusha is the new Covenant, as He promised to write them on our hearts (minds). "'Not by might, nor by power, but by My Spirit' – says Yahuah Tsabaoth." - ZekarYah 4:6

WHAT IS THE LIE?
THE BELIEF THAT OBEDIENCE IS UNNECESSARY
This is the opposite of the renewed Covenant.
 If we *refuse to receive a love for the Truth*, His Torah, then He sends us a strong delusion to believe the lie -- that obedience is unnecessary. This is the secret of *lawlessness*, called the mystery of *iniquity*. Satan used this delusion on the woman in the garden of Eden, leading to disobedience. Simply believing Yahusha died for our sins so that we can continue to disobey and keep on sinning willfully is the very thing Hebrews 10:26-28 directly refutes, as well as the often quoted 10:16, 17.
Yahusha did not come to deliver us from His Torah, but rather its penalty, if we believe and repent (turn away from sin).
First: the message of the Kingdom is *"REPENT, for the reign of Yahuah draws near."* This means to stop sinning, and return, turn back to Torah -- it is a mystery, veiled to those Yahuah does not call. This is the message Yahusha stated again and again. He enables us to love the Commandments by His supernatural power. This is a light yoke, but it comes with worldly costs attached -- persecution for righteousness' sake from highly

religious teaching authorities. The message endangers their control over people's minds, exposing the wormwood they teach. Yahusha's criticism with the leadership concerned the things that were ADDED by human traditions. He did not found or invent a new way at all. Men's traditions became their commandments, just as we see has happened over the centuries until today.
Second: the New Covenant is having the Torah *written on our HEARTS*; this is explained at Jeremiah YirmeYahu 31, Hebrews chapters 8 & 10. The same laws (or more accurately teachings) are written on our hearts by Yahusha's Spirit, _enabling_ us *to LOVE them*. This is what happened for the first time at "Pentecost" **(Shabuoth)**. The circumcision of our heart is pictured by our immersion in water (Kol. 2:11,12), showing our pledge of a good conscience toward Yahuah. He said, ***"If you love Me, keep*** (guard, observe, obey) ***My Commandments."*** When we are convicted of our sinfulness, we are to repent of our sins, and obey. The Torah DEFINES what is a sin at 1 Yn. / John 3:4. Please read 1 Yn. / John 3:22-24, and see if anything harmonizes with what we're discussing here.
Yahuah's Covenant is for any foreigner who joins to Yahuah -- see Isaiah / YashaYahu 56. There is no covenant in Scripture with any people but Israel, and is 12 tribes, not just the "Jews" (Yahudim). Outsiders become fellow citizens through the same Covenant, and are treated as native-born. Those delivered from Egypt were a mixed-multitude of many enslaved peoples, and they became one nation, Yahuah's people.
Israel is Yahuah's wife (or bride). Those *observant* of Shabath / Shabath will be brought to His set-apart mountain, and be among His people (see Is. 56, and 66). Sabbath is the **test**, to see whether or not we will **obey** His Commandments. (Ex. 16:4) Reading Acts, you will see the word "Sabbath" often - and this is not Sun-day. Yahusha is the **"Master of the Shabath,"** yet Christianity outlawed Shabath at the Council of Laodicea (363-365 CE). This alteration of the Word is wormwood, and the world has been feeding on it for over 1600 years.
The act of resting on Shabath is the sign of the eternal Covenant that commemorates CREATION, and shows Yahuah you acknowledge Him as Creator. It marks you as His property as a sign on your hand and His Name seals you for the Day of

Redemption. Try to find in Scripture where legalism (according to Torah, not human traditions) is ever a problem for anyone. Human legalism is rampant -- look at Sun-day, Easter, Christmas, and so on. Easter is Ishtar, the Earth Mother; Christmas was originally the birth of the SUN, and was originally Nimrod's birthday, and all other Sun deities. Santa is Nimrod. These things are invented by men, and are not found anywhere in Scripture. If you don't observe them, you're considered strange. Lawlessness, the ignoring of the Torah (walking in darkness) is our problem, and this is what satan has been so successful in promoting.

You could begin by reading James 1:23, and the entire chapter 2, where belief is perfected by works of obedience. We show our faith by our obedience. This is not in conflict with Ephesians 2, because the gift is our belief, which enables us to do good works, such as observe the Torah (Eph. 2:10). The unconverted human lives in the "mind of the flesh" and interprets the Scriptures seeking out lawlessness from the dark point of view, and will not submit to the Torah of Yahuah, nor can it do so. But, the **mind of the Spirit** enables us to obey, because we AGREE with the Torah, and given a love for it. We are to love the Commandments of Yahuah, and teach them. Yahusha told us that whosoever keeps and teaches them will be called great in the Kingdom, but whosoever annuls the least of them will be the least. Romans chapters 6 through 8 will explain the New Covenant to you. Paul's letters *refine details*, and can easily confuse those who are not taught correctly, as Kefa warned us at 2 Pet.3:15-17. He said the untaught distort the meaning of Paul's letters, and become lawless. Don't fall from your steadfastness. Yahusha is near, ask Him to reveal the Truth to you, and write His perfect Torah on your heart. His thoughts are not our thoughts, so we seek His thoughts, His opinion, and take on His personality. Then, you will begin an incredible task He has prepared just for you to go and teach others all He has commanded, and immerse them into His Name, Yahusha. You will see your teachers (the Commandments), and hear a voice behind you, saying **"This is the way, walk in it."** - YashaYah 30:21 You will love obeying. Your obedience is your way of showing Yahuah you love Him, and is evidence of your being delivered, perfecting your belief. Disobedience and syncretism (mixing) is harlotry. We can't invent our worship - that's what Kain did.

WHEN DID THE CIRCUS BECOME ISRAEL?
Since the 17th century they've been calling it the Church – but we call it the CIRCUS. Church, kirche, and circus come from the same Greek word Kirk, usually referring to a pagan temple! To get rid of the Commandments, especially that "Jewish" Commandment called the Sabbath, they had to get rid of Israel, and pretend the Church is now spiritual Israel. This is called **Replacement Theology**, or Supersessionism. There's no Scripture supporting this idea. We who have been awakened and have overcome by the blood of Yahusha know that the lies are predicated on people believing this Replacement Theology. They are taught they replace Israel and no longer have to obey the Covenant -- the Everlasting Covenant. The TRUE Israel of YaHUaH is the wife/bride of Yahusha, and they "keep the Commandments," and will be able to enter into the gates of the city (New Yerushaliyim). Outside will be those who do not obey, called dogs. These are the lawless and have contempt and bitterness toward obedience, but are filled with religious fervor for everything men invented – all the wormwood they can eat is offered to them every Sunday morning.
http://www.fossilizedcustoms.com/sundayorigins.html

For centuries after the resurrection of Yahusha, false teachers arose to draw away disciples after themselves, just as Paul predicted would occur (Acts 20). Today we look back and call these men the **church fathers**. **www.fossilizedcustoms.com** Pantaenus, Augustine, Tertullian, Jerome, Epiphanius, and a dozen others guided the doctrines, and a great falling-away occurred through these elders (bishops, overseers).
THEY DO NOTHING YAHUAH SAID, AND EVERYTHING HE SAID NOT TO DO
Yahuah tells us **not to learn the ways** of the heathen, nor serve Him in their way (Dt. 12:30-32). Yahusha told us **"Man does not live by bread only, but by EVERY WORD that proceeds from the mouth of Yahuah."**
With this in mind, we see the world learned to do the opposite:
We modify the fertility, and do it like a Hindu anyway;
EGGS, RABBITS, TREES, STEEPLES, STATUES, HOLY WATER, WREATHS, EASTER, CHRISTMAS, SUN-DAY, MONKS, RELICS, BEADS, HALOES, TRINITIES, SACRAMENTS, BELLS, SUNRISE SERVICES,

PROCESSIONS, CRUXES, and more. **They left nothing behind, except everything Yahuah told us to do.**

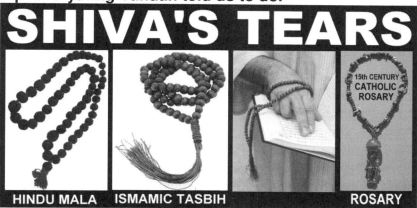

He tells us to rest on the 7th day, so we rest on the 1st day and *work* on the 7th. **He tells us what we may eat;** we tell Him we're going to eat *everything* <u>we</u> want to eat. For more on what food is: **www.fossilizedcustoms.com/food.html**
He tells us to *call on His Name*, Yahuah; instead, we call Him by generic terms, even former pagan proper nouns such as **GOD** or **LORD** (BAAL). They turned His Name into wormwood.
www.fossilizedcustoms.com/name.html

TRANSLITERATIONS			
6,823	216	2	1
YAHUAH	YAHUSHA	YAHUSHUA	Y'SHUA
HEBREW ҙYҙ⅂	OWYҙ⅂	OYWYҙ⅂	OYW⅂
ARAMAIC הוהי	עשוהי	עושוהי	עושי
GREEK IAOUE	IHSOUS		
LATIN IEHOUAH	IESU		

AT HEBREWS 4 AND ACTS 7 THE SAME GREEK LETTERING IS USED
FOR "JOSHUA" AND "JESUS" - IHSOUS
THIS IS CONFIRMATION BOTH WERE CALLED YAHUSHA IN HEBREW
TORAH INSTITUTE

He tells us to observe *specific appointed times*, so we use our own reasoning, mostly based on formerly Pagan observances we've adapted to fit what we want them to mean. We follow men who scorned the Natsarim and wanted nothing in common with the Yahudim, admitted to by their own words.
Yahuah's **festivals** reflect the **redemption plan** for Yisharal, but were forsaken (Dan 7:25). All the nations of the Earth are invited to engraft into the commonwealth of Yisharal through *the*

23

Covenant (Eph. 2:8-13), but it's called legalism when anyone obeys - legalism equates to heresy. If we are legal then we are true citizens of Yisharal; if we practice lawlessness, we are imposters, and usurping what is not ours to claim.

We cannot simultaneously claim to be Yahusha's followers and not obey Torah. If we claim to know Him, then we obey the Commandments (1 Yn. 3).

THE MYSTERY OF LAWLESSNESS

The dragon joined and corrupted doctrines from within by twisting, controlling, and confusing the meaning of all the pagan traditions. Educated men found it difficult to detect what was of human design (humanism, man's way), and what was expected of us from the Words of Scripture. Replacement Theology was a doctrine enforced under pain of death. Natsarim were condemned by the religious teaching authority because they observed the Commmandments and rejected the authority of the Circus. **http://www.fossilizedcustoms.com/mystery.htm**

We obey Yahuah's Commandments because we love Him and know Him. We walk as Yahusha walked, not like a Hindu.

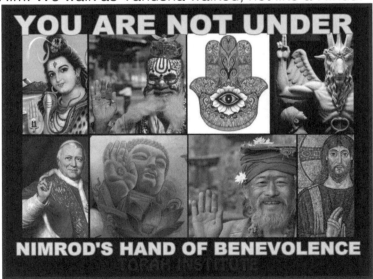

THE LIGHT EXPOSES THE WORMWOOD

Trusting the Word of Yahuah gives us eyesight. Yahuah calls His Word the **"Scripture of Truth"** (Danial 10:21). If we will not receive a love for the **Truth**, He sends a **strong delusion** to

blind us. Hinduism is darkness, and it multiplied Nimrod's rebellion (worship of the host of heaven) into the whole world. Kneeling to images, holy water, pillars, circumambulating, trinities, praying to the dead, beads, repetitious prayers, birthdays (queen of heaven cakes), zodiac/living animals, and other behavior ignites Yahuah's jealous rage. We can feel His rage inside us as we see people defending these things He warned us to avoid. "He knows my heart" is a statement we hear often from a bronze forehead, or "It doesn't mean that to me," as if they are above caring because they worship themselves, not Yahuah. We can never go wrong if we remember the Covenant (Malaki 4:1-6), and stand firmly on that foundation. Ecclesiastes 12:13 and YashaYahu / Isaiah 8:20 puts men's ideas to shame.
http://www.fossilizedcustoms.com/lamp.html

NUMBER THREE UNPACKED:
You do not (**LO** H3808, no, never, not) **cast** (**NASA** H5375, throw) **the Name** (**SHEM** H8034, Name) **of Yahuah** (**YOD-HAY-UAU-HAY** H3068, I was, I am, I will be) **your Alahim** (**ALAHIM** H430, lofty/mighty one) **to ruin** (**SHOAH** H7723, ruin, destruction).

What Is His Name? Proverbs 30:4
His Name Is Like A Fire – YirmeYahu/Jer. 20:9
His Word Is Like A Hammer - YirmeYahu 23:29
YashaYahu/Is. 42:8 reveals the Name of our Creator in four vowels. The one Name (Acts 4:12) given under heaven for deliverance carries the meaning, *I am your Deliverer:* Google YAHUSHA
Yahuah Rafa, Yahuah Yireh, Yahuah Alahim, Yahuah Al Shaddai, Yahuah Nissi, Yahuah Shalom, and other forms share His attributes / roles, but His Name is the same and a memorial to all generations (Shemoth/Ex. 3:15). We cannot cast His Name to ruin by substituting it with devices. Yual / Joel 2:32 and Malaki 3:16-18 reveal how calling on His Name is going to make a distinction one day soon.
http://fossilizedcustoms.com/name.html

BITTER TROLLS
Destroying the reputation of another person is known as trolling when the Internet is used, but in general we never make

ourselves look good when we try to make someone else look bad. Hiding our identity as we attack someone's reputation shows everyone how dark our heart really is.

If we keep Php. 4, Eph. 4, and Romans 12 in mind at all times, we can **identify the fruit** of any tree, including the fruit we are bearing in ourselves. The Torah is a mirror that shows us what we look like as we behave in the world.

May we all reflect Yahusha's essence always.

Forgive as you have been forgiven.

When we see Yahusha's wounds, we will feel in our heart how much He loves us.

NUMBER NINE UNPACKED:

"You do not bear false witness against your neighbor."
You do not (**LO** H3808, no, never, not) **bear** (**ANAH** H6030, testify, announce, utter, propagate) **false** (**SHOA** H7722, devastating, desolating, deceptive, destructive, harmful) **witness** (**ED** H5707, testify, record, words) **against your neighbor** (**REYA** H7453, associate, fellow, companion). We don't seek to damage or ruin our neighbor. Literally, it means **"You do not bear harmful speech against your neighbor,"** or **"You do not propagate harmful words about your neighbor."** The principle behind this and other Commandments is the **"Golden Rule."**
This is training in how to love our neighbor, even our enemies.
"Therefore, whatever you wish men to do to you, do also to them, for this is the Torah and the Prophets." - Mt. 7:12
In either side of a matter, a "spin" can be formed to justify one's perspective. It helps to play scary music and conceal one's identity as the attacker projects their perspective, but then Proverbs 18:17 shows us this: **"The first to state his own case seems right, until another comes and examines him."**
The bearer of an evil report, or one trying to make someone else look bad (as we see in politics constantly) transmits words of death that are intended to destroy the reputation of another person. One day we'll all see the wounds we caused because we chose not to love.
By His wounds we are healed - YashaYahu 53:5
Galatians 4:9-11 is misunderstood by the Alexandrian culture of lawless wormwood. Paul was writing to converts who were settling back to their old festivals, such as birthdays, Sun/fertility

festivals like Dec. 25th and Easter. The festivals of Yahuah and His Shabath are not **weak and miserable**, but are eternal.

The Nimrod reign will end when Yahusha returns, and I hope you will take a second look at what Paul was writing about, and to whom. God-worship began with Nimrod, the first to become a *mighty-one* in the Earth. Look up the definition of the word GOD on the Internet. Yahuah is the Possessor of Heaven and Earth, and is our Alahim.

People are programmed to think lawlessly. The **yoke** which their fathers could not bear (Gal. 2:11-14) was the traditions of the fathers, which Paul said was his former life in Yahudaism (rabbinic). Torah is our first love, which we have departed from because of the lawless teachers of Alexandria (circus fathers). They invented their own teachings, abandoning the old paths. Keep using Scripture, but be aware there are many centuries of twisting it before we awakened:

1 Timothy 1:5-7 shows what Torah is about:

"Now the goal of this command is love from a clean heart, from a good conscience and a sincere belief, which some, having missed the goal, turned aside to senseless talk, wishing to be teachers of Torah, understanding neither what they say nor concerning what they strongly affirm."

The most successful way to help the zombies is to tell them they're dead. They are dead because they don't have life, just as darkness is only the absence of light, cold is only the absence of heat, and hatred is only the absence of love.

Their mind of the flesh holds them imprisoned by their own desires. Sin keeps them dead, and there are two kinds: unintentional and intentional. They are so dead they don't care which kind they commit until we can help them appreciate the perspective of Yahusha (Mind of the Spirit). We are so filled with false teachings it is necessary to purge all things men made up that Scripture doesn't mention.

From that newly emptied wineskin (mind), we can pour-in the essential thing they were taught to repel:

The Everlasting Covenant of kindness (kasid).

With what we planted into them, we can trust Yahusha will help them learn to love the instructions that train them how to love.

Most would not recognize the true message of deliverance because they have been lulled into a deep sleep by the Gospel of Lawlessness. Due to lawlessness, love has grown cold. They care nothing about living by the Word, and have invented their own name for the one they serve. "LORD" may as well be exactly what it refers to: Nimrod, the original rebel against Yahuah and obedience to Him.

"For You Have Made Great Your Word, Your Name, Above All." - Psalm 138:2

The Word and the Name are what we guard, and one meaning of Natsarim is "guardians." Obedience is better than sacrifice, yet those obeying the Covenant have been ridiculed as legalists, a term equivalent to heretics. The Word **"Jesus"** is not Hebrew, but is a christogram form invented by mystagogues: IESV, and found originally in the Latin Vulgate. The KJV used IESV for the term in 1611, while the Geneva used **IESVS** for the first time in 1599. Both were following the *Latin Vulgate* by Eusebius Sophronius Hieronymus (called "Jerome"). The Name "Yahusha" means "I am your Deliverer." Jesus has no meaning, but stands in place of the true and only Name of our Mashiak. He only has one Name, and it's Hebrew, not Korean or Greek.

REVISIONISM

The record of history is altered constantly. The collective memory is controlled by **traditions**, and the source of those traditions seems unimportant. All that matters is that the traditions are performed by everyone without question.

It's Time For The Natsarim To Shout - YirmeYahu / Jer. 31:6

Is Yahusha's Name like a burning fire shut up in your bones? The anti-mashiak has overtaken most hearts with a false message of complacency, but time is growing short. Those who are receiving a love for the Truth are being sealed in the Name of Yahusha for the Day of Redemption. It's time to shout.

The Covenant of love is an eternal one, instructing us in how to love Yahuah and love our neighbor, even our enemies. If anyone ever tempts us to disobey this Covenant of lovingkindness and to worship another, or comes bearing a message in any other name, we are warned by Yahuah to not listen to him.

The Torah's goal is love, and is not difficult. Through the power of Yahusha, we can do all things. The only worship Yahuah accepts is obedience to His Covenant.

The Covenant is our marriage, the Living Words, and we will celebrate that Covenant with Yahusha at the Marriage Supper of the Lamb.

We are sealed for that day in the one Name given under heaven: Yahusha. We obey the Commandments of Yahuah, and we hold to the testimony of Yahusha.

The 5 unwise virgins are still sleeping; let's wake up as many as we can. Google YAHUSHA - this Name will take Babel down one day soon.

We are the hunters, and the zombies are all around us.

"'See, I am sending for many fishermen,' declares Yahuah, 'and they shall fish them. And after that I shall send for many hunters, and they shall hunt them from every mountain and every hill, and out of the holes of the rocks.'"

- YirmeYahu 16:16 BYNV

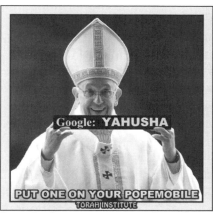

When it dawns on you that Constantine altered the 4th Commandment and Yahusha's idea of the 7th day will never be **Sun-day**, the influx of Truth will paralyze you for a few moments as He comes into you. This is how it happens for all of us.

The reason we received the strong delusion in the first place was because we would not receive a love for the Truth, and obey from our heart. Pursue the Truth (with all your heart), and He will do the rest by revealing Himself to you.

THE SIGN OF THE EVERLASTING COVENANT

A wise manager feeds the sheep the Commandments.

The 7th day is **still blessed** from creation week, but the world thinks otherwise. It's the **sign** of the **everlasting Covenant** - Exo 31:15-17:
'Six days work is done, and on the seventh is a Shabath of rest, set-apart to Yahuah. Everyone doing work on the Shabath day shall certainly be put to death.
And the children of Yisharal shall guard the Shabath, to observe the Shabath throughout their generations as an everlasting Covenant.
Between Me and the children of Yisharal it is a sign forever. For in six days Yahuah made the heavens and the earth, and on the seventh day He rested and was refreshed.'
Yahuah spent 40 years re-training them about the Shabath using manna, not the moon. The annual Shabath days involve the moon, but not the weekly Shabath days.

"And I also gave them My Shabaths, to be a sign between them and Me, to know that I am Yahuah who sets them apart." - Eze 20:12 (See also YashaYahu / Isaiah 56 and Malaki 4:1-6)
What we call something may not be what it is in reality.
The day of the Sun is not the Shabath anymore than a covenant between a turtle and a woman is a marriage.

LORD OF THIS WORLD
Our Words Need To Be Precise. The **"Lord of this world"** is a phrase well understood by most people. The world hears the word *Lord* and thinks whatever they have been programmed to understand. **Lord Krishna** is "Ravi" in Hindi. Ravi is the title for their sun deity, Surya, and means "Lord." To them, Krishna is the sun deity. The 1st day of their week is called RAVIVARA, or the "Lord's Day." Sunday (the day of the sun) is accepted as the "Lord's Day." The true Name of our Creator, Who blessed the 7th day as a remembrance of His rest (Hebrews 4) has a name. Psalm 23 begins with His Name: **"Yahuah is my Shepherd."**
If the **LORD** is our shepherd, then **Baal** is our shepherd.
Look up the title Baal, also used as the term for the sun deity in many cultures (pagan cults). Baal means "LORD."
YashaYahu / Isaiah 42: 8 tells us His Name is Yahuah.
The destruction of the true Name, Yahuah, goes against the 1st, 2nd, and 3rd Commandments. The replacement day of rest, Sunday, was done by Constantine (321 CE), and goes against the

4th Commandment. Guarding the last 6 Commandments (which teach us how to love our neighbor) is a fine thing to teach. But if we disregard the first 4 that teach us how to love Yahuah, the early circus fathers have done us a disservice. The 7th day is still blessed, and Constantine does not need our obedience.
We are servants of the one we obey, so we need to be precise in both word and deed, and not consume wormwood.

"The good man brings forth what is good from the good treasures of his heart, and the wicked man brings forth what is wicked from the wicked treasure.
And I say to you that for every idle word men speak, they shall give an account of it in the day of judgment.
For by your words you shall be declared righteous, and by your words you shall be declared unrighteous." – Mt. 12:35-37

RECOGNIZING SHEPHERDS WHO TELL THE TRUTH
"So Yahusha said to those Yahudim who believed Him,
'If you abide in My Word, you are truly My taught ones, and you shall know the Truth, and the Truth shall make you free.'" - Yn 8:31-32

"And I shall give you shepherds according to My heart, and they shall feed you with knowledge and understanding."
- YirmeYahu 3:15

"Let the words of my mouth and the meditation of my heart be pleasing before You, O Yahuah, my Rock and my Redeemer." - Psalm 19:14

Imagine a young shepherd boy named Daud as he was guarding his flock under a clear night sky.
He used his **rod** to guide the strays, and weilded his **staff** as a weapon against predators that might attack them.
Looking into the vastness of space, he realized another
level far above him, where Yahuah was like a shepherd to him:

"Yahuah is my shepherd; nothing do I need.
He makes me to lie down in green pastures;
He leads me beside still mayim.
He restores my breath;
He leads me in paths of uprightness for His Name's sake."
Psalm 23:1-3 (BYNV) SEEK THE ANCIENT PATHS - BE RESTORED TO FAVOR

INSIGHTS INTO THE WORLD ORDER OF THE BEAST

When I was a child being trained by the Jesuits, they openly explained how the world system's power structure is organized. Since **Babel**, the world has been organized in this beast system, or order. It is a highly-ordered **teaching authority**, controlling and wielding power over the commoners, whom they refer to as the **laity** (common people).

The dragon gives them this authority and power.

We often hear non-professionals referred to as *lay-people*, or *laity*. This term implies there are more informed people who were in **control**.

The **Jesuit-Illuminati** was all around me, but only later did I become aware of their presence and strategies. The only organized **teaching authorities** they recognize is *theirs*; all others were evil. Theirs was the only means to attain (or earn) "heaven" and the other teaching authorities had to be opposed and totally eliminated. **The Jesuits are a military order which rose up to resist the Reformation. They seek to restore the papacy to it's former position of power over the world.**

This militia is a totalitarian, organized government *posing as a religious institution*. Its greatest operation is the **United Nations**. This is a foreign power entrenched on the sovereign soil of the United States.

It is a foothold that so far remains unrecognized.

The *3 estates* of the world order are the way the dragon controls us. Once an insider, I was taught the order of world powers:

1. **The Clergy** (papacy, cardinals, priests)
2. **The Nobility** (all governmental levels)
3. **The Commoners**, or **laity**, the people living out in the sticks (city dwellers, and the *pagus*, woodland dwellers having quaint superstitions).

The Latin term *pagus* (forest-dweller) became our modern word *pagan*. They had a reputation for holding to primitive beliefs, so the term *pagus* was highly derogatory. This book will change everything: with the Truth.

The ignorance of the pagans (Latin, *pagus*) was exploited in the past, only now they are called "*lay people*" – being the ignorant masses.

After the printing press was invented in the early 15th century, the *media* slowly became what is referred to as a **4th estate**.

It became a powerful authority, and attempts to **control**

information. The teaching authority of the clergy is constantly being exposed and challenged by the Truth. The collision between Truth and tradition is on display every day in the media.

CONSTANTINE COINS WITH HIS DEITY APOLLO

CONSTANTINE: THE FATHER OF CHRISTIANITY

ROMAN TIME IS WORMWOOD

Doctrine means *teaching*. It's a Latin word, related to ***document*** (a written instruction). The Latin word **Doctor** means *teacher*. We've been programmed from birth with various traditions, rituals, and customs. All paganism is targeted at children.

How we keep track of **time** is a world-wide type of programming. Here we will look into how we came to be trained to think of and organize time ~ in our ***days, months, and years***.

The first thing we do when we awaken each day is check the **time**. Originally, the **hours** of daylight were measured using a **sundial**, and the shadow of the sun marked off 12 hours *(horo)* until it set. ***Horoscopos*** means *hour-watcher*. The marked hours on the sundial pass more quickly in the winter months, and slower in the summer months. There was no "daylight-saving-time" trick to deal with, the length of the hours measured on the sundial varied in length. There were always 12 hours of daylight. What we call ***noon*** is the Latin ***nones*** (meaning 9). It was the 9th hour after sunrise, or 3 p.m. in the ancient world.

Each day of the week was originally referred to by a **number**. The 7th day also had a name: *Shabath*, meaning **rest, cease**. Adam and Kuah, the first man and woman, observed the 7-day week. There is no one named Eve in the Hebrew text; this name was embraced to appease pagans because one of the names for their Earth Mother was Eve.

The name Kuah is derived from the Hebrew word **Kai**, meaning ***life*** ~ thus her name means mother of the living. The ending *–ah*

33

renders it feminine, similar to the ending in *Sharah*. Shar means prince, or ruler; *Sharah* means princess. You will notice the days of the week have been given **names**. The names were taken from among pagans who honored their deities by **calling the days by the names of their idols.**

SABBATH - SHIN-BETH-TAU: "**Shabath**"
Shatan altered the day of rest to the pagan Dies Solis (Day of the Sun) in 321 (the Edict of Constantine).
Since that time the world has thought of the original Shabath as the Roman day of Saturn, or "Satyr Day."
What day of the week followed the 7th day (Barashith / Genesis 2:3)?
It wasn't the **8th day**, it was the **1st day**, beginning another cycle over again. A "week" of seven days in Hebrew is "SHABUA," a word based on the meaning of "seven" - SHEBA. This cycle of seven is seen throughout Scripture. 7 intact weeks add-up to 49 days, as we see prescribed at Lev. 23:15, & Dt. 16:9, and modeled in *years* at Lev. 25:8. What day followed the 7th day isn't dependent on anything created during the first 7 days as some have proposed using the moon phases. The **week** is its own independent creation of time, determined by counting the days to the 7th day (a sign of rest). Yahuah re-trained His people in the wilderness by providing a double-portion of manna on the 6th day, and none on the 7th. Shatan molested it as prophesied at Danial 7:25, and now that people are returning (teshubah) to the correct day, people are trying to blame the 7-day cycle on the Romans, and writing books about it - but not citing Scripture. They twist Scripture to force things into the meaning to draw away talmidim after themselves. They teach doctrines of demons.

SUN-DAY (day 1)
From Latin, *dies Solis*, the *Day-of-the-Sun*. Since Babylon was established, pagans have worshipped the **Sun**.
Here's a few of the names they've used: Baal (LORD), Bel, Shamash, Molok, Ahura-Mazda, Dagon, Sol, Marduk, Mithras, Krishna, Amon-Ra, Aton, Woden (Odin, Adonis), Zeus, Deus, and the Druid / Teutonic "**God**." You'll recall the **Pharaoh** and the **Kaisar** (Caesar) (Khazar/Czar) were worshipped as the **sun's offspring**. This pattern began with the first king, **Nimrod**.

WORSHIP OF THE HEAVENLY HOST

The worship of the sun, moon, planets, and stars was the pattern for the Babylonians, Persians, Chaldeans, Egyptians, Greeks, Romans, Celts, Mayans, Aztecs, and Indians. They were turned-over to worship the **host of heaven** (mazzaroth – see Acts 7:42). The governments were the religion. If they were *good pagans*, at death they would be transported to the skies (Heaven) to live with their deities. This was called Nirvana, Shambala, or Elysian Fields. The Roman Consul/Emperor **Constantine I** gave us the term **Sun-Day**, which referred to the day honoring Sol Invictus Mithras (the unconquerable sun, Mithras). This Mithras was the Persian term for Apollo. Here's a coin minted by Constantine showing Apollo and Constantine together:

CONSTANTINE & APOLLO

TORAH INSTITUTE

In 321 CE he decreed under the penalty of death that all artisans, merchants, and people of his Empire cease work on the Venerable **Day of the Sun**, to honor Mithras/Apollo. This was a Universal Edict, and is still enforced in our western culture with our blue laws. Interestingly, the **government phone numbers** are printed on blue pages in our US phone books. It was a weekly ritual of sun-worshippers to assemble at dawn on this day to greet the sun at its rising. A great **pillar**, or sun-ray **obelisk** was the solar religion's primitive high place, condemned as a "pillar of jealousy" ~ secretly (esoterically) interpreted as a male fertility symbol. Tower designs such as steeples, pagodas, turrets, ziggurats, minarets, spires, obelisks, and pyramids are forbidden by Yahuah.

The Temple did not have a high place, nor do any buildings where Yahuah's people come together. **Sacred pillars** of jealousy were to be demolished - Yahuah hates them.

These pagan high places would receive the first hallowed rays of

dawn. In the primitive cultures, **bells** were rung by hand, as in a shaker-grid, and large ones were struck with oak logs swung horizontally. Gongs struck with hammers were especially fun for the Oriental pagan, but they also used the familiar bell shape too. In the book, *The Conquest of Peru*, Prescott is an eye-witness to blatant sun-worship: ***"The Inca would assemble at dawn eagerly. They watched the coming of the deity, and no sooner did his first yellow rays strike the turrets, than a shout of gratulation broke forth from the assembled multitude, the wild tunes from barbaric instruments swelled louder and louder as his bright orb shone in full splendor on his votaries."***
http://www.fossilizedcustoms.com/sundayorigins.html

The Romans considered anyone who did not worship the sun to be an atheist and a traitor, since Kaiser was the sun enthroned in a man. **Foreign beliefs** found some tolerance in the Edict of Milan, 313 CE. Religion, politics, and sports were all different facets of the same thing:
a means of controlling the behavior of a captive population.
A nation can be thought of as a huge neighborhood gang, but with boundaries that end where another gang's boundaries begin. Thugs rule all the citizens.
If you get out of line, those in control feel their power over you slipping. Sun-day is one of their biggest promotions.

MOON DAY (day 2)
The Old English term was monan daeg, as translated from Latin, where **mona** means moon. *Mona Lisa* means **moon lily**. We get our word **month** (moonth) from **mona**, the 29.5 day orbital cycle, but this 2nd weekday is named what it is because it has been dubbed the **moon's day**. The moon was identified with Artemis (Diana), and in some cults the sun and moon were the *eyes of heaven*. Artemis is depicted with the crescent moon beneath her feet as if riding in a boat ~ exactly as you will see Miryam (Mary) in Roman Catholic illustrations. The *Astral King*,

the sun, and his sister the moon, were the dominant figures that shaped the astro-biological mind. The **futility** of honoring Pagan deities was because their foolish hearts were darkened.

They did not honor or give thanks to the Creator, though His invisible attributes are clearly seen.

TUES-DAY (day 3)

Tyr's Day: "day of Tiu." Teutonic Druid-Celtic idol. The population of the Angles and Saxons were kept under control by various Druid priest cults. Like any other Pagan religion, the population lived in fear and ignorance, while the **parasite** fed off of them and kept them brain-washed. Druids still worship the sun at Stonehenge every Summer Solstice. Tyr, or Tiu, was the Norse deity of **war,** considered the son of Odin (Woden).

The French call this day **Mardi** (Mar's Day), after Mars, the Roman's deity of war! **Mardi Gras** is the French name for *fat Tuesday*, still bearing the name of the Roman deity. This festival falls the day before *Ash Wednesday*, the beginning of **Lent**, both to be discussed later.

WEDNES-DAY (day 4) **Celtic Crux symbol** (solar). This day comes from another pagan idol's name. An elder in Iceland couldn't stand it anymore, and changed the days back to numbers for that island several hundred years ago. When we say it's "Wednesday" (Woden, Odin), we are declaring it to be *Woden's Day*. Considered highly skilled in magic (majik), this Celtic deity was, to the Teutonic pagan, the husband of Freya, or Frigga. The Romans honored Mercury on this day, calling it *Mercurii dies* (Mercury's Day).

This mid-week evening was highly regarded as a night of majik. Druids met to hold hands in a **circle**, chant, enchant, cast spells, and do it while surrounding a **burning cross**, the symbol of Woden (Odin). The Celtic crux is a pagan majik symbol, the Trifolium clover leaf representing Woden, Frigga, and Thor.

Other Druid trinities included Esus, Teutates, & Taranus. Anglo-Saxon xenophobia (fear of foreigners) and Druid customs are seen today in the modern Ku Klux Klan. They still call their leaders **wizards** and use the Celtic term *Klan*, a traditional social unit in Scot Land. The word comes from the Greek ***kuklos***, meaning ***circle***. The name Circe is related to CIRCUS (church).
They like circles, cruxes, and sometimes Druid costumes.

DID YAHUAH TELL US TO DO THIS?

The **Klan** - a very secretive society, rose up mainly in the South (US) after the civil war, to reassert white supremacy by terroristic methods. The Druids were very nationalistic, so it was difficult for Rome to conquer them. The only way Christianity could win them over was to absorb their culture.
This is called inculturation, or **syncretism**.
Syncretism: the attempt to reconcile or combine differing beliefs in philosophy or religion by uniting them; mixing two or more behaviors together. The expression, "on the surface," indicates there is something concealed. Is this the real reason some Christians meet together on this night? Catholics have always had a ***novena*** session on this night, intended for "new converts" to be trained.
Woden's emblem was the Celtic Crux, a cross with the **circle** (the sun). No wonder we see so many pictures of crosses with the sun nimbus behind it, and sunsets in Christian art — not to mention the ***halos*** of yellow around the heads of "Jesus" and the

"saints." This will be shown to be a world-wide pagan influence; Buddha, Krishna, Ahura-Mazda, and Jupiter are just a few found with haloes.

CHRISTIANOS – The Origin Of The Word Christian

Christian / Christians is only used a total of 3 times in all of Scripture, and it is only in the Greek **translation**. The word *Christianity* is not found.

In the ancient setting, it was a term of scorn used by the Greeks to indicate a person was slow, or retarded.

We get our word **cretin** from the Greek word, *christianos*. A dictionary defines cretin [kret'n]: "a fool; and idiot. French **cretin**, idiot; from Swiss French, crestin, CHRISTIAN."

We will examine the word **Christian** and its use in the Greek world later.

For now, let it be enough to say that the sect which was established by the true Mashiak was called **Natsarim** (see Acts 24:5).

THOR

THOR'S DAY

THURS-DAY (day 5)

The Celtic Thor's Day; the deity of thunder and son of Woden and Freya. The same as Taranus, Thor was associated with thunder; the Dutch donder, or Germanic donner (one of Santa's reindeer). The Romans honored Jupiter on this day, which was originally **IU-PITAR**, meaning Jovis-father. *Jove* corresponds to Zeus. The altar of Zeus, used at every Olympic game, is lit by a torch. The altar is shaped like a "**T**."

Thor's emblem was the hammer, secretly interpreted as the letter "**T**," referring to **Tammuz** (Babylonian Duzu), the son of Nimrod and Semiramis. Zeus was originally pronounced *DZEUS*.

FRIGGA - CELTIC NAME FOR THE GREAT MOTHER
FRI-DAY (day 6)

Old English, Frigedaeg, this was Frey Day or Frigga Day. **Frigga** was the wife of Woden. The fertility concept associated with this day is very ancient. The Greeks honored **Aphrodite** on this day, and the Romans venerated **Venus** (Astarte). This day was the Egyptian's day of **Isis**, depicted with the symbol of the fish on her head. The **fish** symbol pre-dates the Egyptians, coming from the Philistine cult of **Dagon** (Jdg. 16:23, 1Sa. 5:2).

You've seen images of Dagon portrayed as a sea nymph:

STARBUCKS IS PROUD OF THEIR NYMPH SYMBOL

Dag is Hebrew for fish, and the Latin is *Pisces*. It was chosen by Pagans because a female fish lays hundreds, sometimes thousands, of eggs ~ a symbol of fertility. The Romans believed Venus (Astarte) came from the sky in a huge egg (not a saucer). We'll go into more detail when we study the Great Mother, Queen of Heaven (Asherah). Frigga's emblems were also mistletoe and the FISH, and is seen today because Roman Catholics **incultured** this into avoiding red meat on this day, replacing it with fish. They have the "fish fry" (even the word "fry" is describing a young fish). The **Great Mother** (Magna Mater) was universally represented by the fish emblem. The Greek word **ichthys** (ikthus) spelled iota, chi, theta, upsilon, sigma spells **IXTHYS** (fish).

IXTHUS - FISH

ICHTHYS (**IXTHUS**) doesn't mean Christ. It is Greek for *fish*. With considerable craft, the fish has become a Christian symbol due to a Greek anagram designed to utilize the Greek anagram IXTHYS.

ΙΧθΥΣ - ANAGRAM

Iesous Christos Theou Huios Soter

IHS, IC XC - CHRISTOGRAMS

It's a man-made tradition, and it just spells **fish**.

The use of Christograms, or theonyms to stand in place of a name of a deity, was a custom used by mystagogues.

They **encrypted** the Name.

Pagans held-back the names of their deities. Other forms used have been **IC-XC**, **IES**, **IESOUS**, **IESV**, and **IHS**.

In the east, they used **IC-XC**; in the west, IHS as the cryptogram.

YAHUSHA means **YAHUAH** *[I AM]* **YOUR DELIVERER**.

The **sign** of the Mashiak isn't a crux or a fish, but a lampstand (**menorah**) Rev. 1&2. The Hebrew menorah has 7 lamps, and represents His body, the **7 assemblies**, through which flows the living water (lamp oil, the laws which give light to the world).

At Rev. 2:5 He said He would remove the **menorah** if they did not repent (stop being lawless).

Have you noticed any menorahs in any Christian homes or meeting houses? He never threatened to remove any fish.

SATYR-DAY

SATUR-DAY (day 7)

This was the Greco-Roman **Day of Saturn**.

Saturn was the Romans' deity of agriculture, corresponding to the Greeks' deity Cronus. This day was dedicated to Saturnus, as was the big party at the end of the Roman year at the

Solstice, Saturnalia. Satur Day was also called Sater Day, and is unmistakenly linked to other Greco-Roman mythology. The SATYR, a goat-legged half-man with horns and pointed ears, was believed to be a drunken, lecherous demon with an abnormal sexual appetite.

The 7th day and the festival of "Satyrnalia" was modeled perfectly after the satyr profile; mischievousness, drunkenness, and orgiastic revelry.

As you consider the wild week-ends enjoyed today by dating couples and party animals with their "mojo" drives, it's clear nothing has changed.

The Greek letter **Y** is upsilon, our letter "**U**".

Here's a big foundational girder with no rivets, installed by **Constantine** in the Roman year 321 CE. This 7th day, the commemoration of Creation in which we honor the Creator as the Creator is a *Temple in time* from sunset "Frey Day" to sunset "Satyr Day" ~ changed to his "Sun-Day" under penalty of death, by only the authority of a man. All theologians and scholars admit there is no Scriptural basis for this change, but it was done by the authority of "the Church." **Shabath** is the "sign" of the everlasting Covenant, indicating who **we** worship, but most refuse the Covenant. This day which was *set-apart* (dedicated) at Creation to be a day of complete rest from work has been superseded by **traditions** that served to unite pagans together, and overwhelm the beloved of Yahusha, the Natsarim sect. Constantine's historian, Eusebius, records the Emperor's edict: "All things what so ever that is was duty to do on the **Shabath**, these **WE** have transferred to the Lord's Day." He also recorded Constantine's infuriated words, "The cursed wretches who killed our Lord . . . (the Italian Romans executed Him, Constantine's people) . . . We will have NOTHING in common with the hostile rabble of the Yahudim (Jews)." Remember, the Romans executed Yahusha for sedition. Yahusha admitted He was a king, and Kaiser ruled as the king over all the spiritual and secular realm, **depicted in the two fingers** raised by the pope.

No other ruler uses this unique hand gesture.

It is also seen on the **statue of Jupiter** at the Vatican.

The statue was renamed *Peter*. The lifting of two fingers represents the authority to rule sovereignly over both temporal and spiritual realms.

YAHUSHA'S LIFE
BEGAN AT CONCEPTION
TORAH INSTITUTE

What's A Good Hebrew Word For Virgin?

People like to argue about whether or not Miryam was a virgin, or that she fits the prophecy at YashaYahu (Is.) 7:14.

The prophet used the word ALMAH to describe the mother of the coming Mashiak.

It's more than obvious that young unmarried women were virgins, and the ancient Hebrew words for virgin are BETHULAH and ALMAH. ALMAH and BETHULAH are synonyms, and translated interchangeably into Greek as PARTHENOS.

The Hebrew word BATH means daughter, and is related to the word BETHULAH. BETHULAH has been accepted to be exclusively the word meaning virgin, yet this is not true. It really means "small woman," referring to a female child.

Both ALMAH and BETHULAH are great to refer to a sexually-pure young female, and the debate is really about the virginity of Miryam.

We know Miryam was the young woman (ALMAH) referred to in the prophecy, and that she was a virgin by her own admission:

"And Miryam said to the messenger, "How shall this be, since I do not know a man?" - Luke 1:34

She was untouched and pure as she spoke to the messenger Gabrial. Why would Yahuah send Gabrial to a young girl that was in any other condition to make a body for Himself to inhabit? Miryam had several other children after Yahusha, her first-born Son.

There are millions who have never studied who do not know this.

ONCE-SAVED ALWAYS-SAVED WORMWOOD

To the Torah and to the witness! If they do not speak according to this Word, it is because they have no daybreak." - YashaYahu (Is.) 8:20

Leavening (men's teachings) can be subtle and alluring deceptions. A brother was sensing something wrong about what he was being taught, and asked if this doctrine is true or false: Questions like this, and predestination, concern the sovereign judgment of Yahuah, and we know He delivers whomever He wants.

Bearing this in mind, there is also this statement He makes which tells us we can choose to fall away and stop loving Him at any point, and the consequences will be catastrophic for us:

"But when a righteous one turns away from his righteousness and does unrighteousness, according to all the abominations that the wrong one has done, shall he live? All his righteousness which he has done shall not be remembered. For his trespass which he has committed, and for his sin which he has committed, for them he shall die."

- Eze 18:24

"For it is impossible for those who were once enlightened, and have tasted the heavenly gift, and have become partakers of the Set-apart Spirit, and have tasted the good Word of Alahim and the powers of the age to come, and fall away, to renew them again to repentance – having impaled for themselves the Son of Alahim again, and put Him to open shame." – Hebrews 6:4-6

The maxim **"once saved always saved"** is a lie from the father of lies. There are so many doctrines of demons we have to stay vigilant at all times.

At Acts 21 the converts were instructed beyond the "four essentials," and to continue their learning by listening to Mosheh read aloud in the congregations "**every Shabath.**"

What could that phrase, "every Shabath" be about?

CASUISTRY WORMWOOD: ARE YOU A VICTIM?

"See, I send you out as sheep in the midst of wolves. Therefore be wise as serpents and innocent as doves."

- Mt. 10:16 BYNV

Cases or **case-studies** are used all the time in **debates**.

44

We are all familiar with the concept of having two sides to any argument, and in the process of arriving at Truth we use these three stages of debate (the Greek word for debate is dialektike):
Thesis - an idea is presented, not yet known to be true.
Anti-Thesis - an opposing idea is presented to challenge the validity of the Thesis.
Synthesis - The conflict resolution reconciling the common truths of the thesis and anti-thesis, starting the process over again. In philosophy this 3-stage process is called the Hegelian Dialectic.

Jesuit-Illuminati brain-washing techniques use several techniques that program the thought processes, but their methods back-fired as they used them on me.

Do not believe their **logical fallacies**. Often teachers will attempt to use a logical fallacy to prove their **thesis**, and you can recognize this Jesuit tactic by the entanglement they are trying to force on your thinking. It may sound plausible, but it's a lie.

They will accuse others of being the wolf-in-sheep's-clothing, as they describe exactly *what they are doing themselves.*

Infiltrating teachers will approach a study not from the ***Hebrew roots,*** but with the words used in common translations, such as the word "LORD." They will attempt to construct a "case" based on equivocating words, phrases, maxims, or ideology.

This approach is called **casuistry**, and is a common Jesuit tactic, and employs sophistry, along with the use of clever but unsound reasoning, especially in relation to moral questions. They attempt to deceive using fallacious theological reasoning.

THE TRUTH WILL JUDGE US

People will often accuse us of judging them because our words show them the Truth. The Truth is what will judge all of us. None of us need to feel judged by anyone but the righteous Judge, Yahusha. There will be no one named "Jesus" doing any judging however. The prophet ZefanYah foretold that our lips would be purified one day (3:9). If there is nothing wrong with our lips (language), then such purification would not be necessary.

YirmeYahu 16:16-19 is very appropriate to this debate:
"'See, I am sending for many fishermen,' declares Yahuah, 'and they shall fish them. And after that I shall send for many hunters, and they shall hunt them from every

mountain and every hill, and out of the holes of the rocks. For My eyes are on all their ways; they have not been hidden from My face, nor has their crookedness been hidden from My eyes. And first I shall repay double for their crookedness and their sin, because they have defiled My land with the dead bodies of their disgusting things, and have filled My inheritance with their abominations.' O Yahuah, my strength and my stronghold and my refuge, in the yom of distress the gentiles shall come to You from the ends of the arets and say, 'Our fathers have inherited only falsehood, futility, and there is no value in them.'" - YirmeYahu 16:16-19

WHAT IS WITCHCRAFT, AND WHO IS GOD?
Witchcraft Is As Witchcraft Does. All rebellion follows the NWO policies (Nimrod World Order). Rebellion is the defining feature of witchcraft, and includes Nimrod's main objective: to give all credit to man's achievements, not to Yahuah.
Any excuse to disobey Yahuah's Covenant of lovingkindness is employed to make the masses feel they are safe from the consequences of their rebellion.
They are told that obedience is impossible, even though Scripture tells us it is not difficult, and we can do all things through Yahusha.

WHO IS GOD?
Nimrod is the first man to be worshipped as GOD. God-worship is not the same as obeying Yahuah, since "In God We Trust" is a motto / maxim of dedication to the Nimrod World Order.
The origin of the term GOD is found in the 1945 Encyclopedia Americana:
"GOD (god) Common Teutonic word for personal object of religious worship, formerly applicable to super-human beings of heathen myth; on conversion of Teutonic races to Christianity, term was applied to Supreme Being."
Nimrod was the original "super-human being," a Super-man. Nimrod is expressed in so many ways it is like seeing a Coca-Cola commercial; they're so pervasive we hardly notice them anymore. **http://www.fossilizedcustoms.com/nimrod.html**

The Superman logo is a red serpent – A God-Man

PaRDeZ - 4 Levels of Interpretation? (Kabbalah wormwood)

The 4 levels of interpretation (or PaRDeZ) is not a teaching from Scripture, but rather comes from Hinduism's Bhagavad Gita and Smriti by way of Kabbalism. Many Hindu practices came along the trade route out of India via the "Silk Road" in the 2nd century BCE. The teachings also affected the Arabs, with crescents, stars, shrines to walk around, and the touchstone which is really a shivalingam and yoni. For more research on this wormwood:
www.fossilizedcustoms.com/kabbalah.html

www.fossilizedcustoms.com/allah.html

VERBAL BATTLES

Arguments over words cause divisions. New strongholds (false reasoning, equivocation, casuistry) are arising among the Natsarim.

"Remind them of this, earnestly witnessing before the Master, not to wage verbal battles – which is useless – to the overthrowing of the hearers. Do your utmost to present yourself approved to Yahuah, a worker who does not need to be ashamed, rightly handling the Word of Truth. But keep away from profane, empty babblings, for they go on to more wickedness, and their word shall eat its way like gangrene. Humenaios and Philetos are of this sort, who have missed the goal concerning the Truth, saying that the resurrection has already taken place, and overthrow the belief of some."
- 2 Timothy 2:14-18

BLOOD, BLESSED, BLESSING

Yahusha's followers have corrected many things our fathers had corrupted. Our lips are being purified (ZefanYah 3:9).

Some teachings only strain to condemn the use of everyday words, without edification or love.

A new trend has arisen promoting the idea that words like bless, blessed, and blessing are evil words because pagans use them, and that the word is based on the word blood. Does this also imply that we should not use the word blood? We must not stand by idly and watch others shoot themselves in the foot. Yahuah does not want us to take the names of foreign deities on our lips (Ex. 23:13, Ps. 16:4). How does this apply to words that are not such names? Videos with scary music and images are popping up on the Internet telling people to avoid the use of words deemed inappropriate.

The Truth will set us free from such false reasoning.

The *Ockham's razor* approach is to eliminate all non-essentials, and keep it as simple as possible.

The Hebrew word AMAN is spelled with 3 letters: ALEF-MEM-NUN. The feminine form is AMANAH, usually translated to mean faith, faithful, faithfulness, steady, steadfast. The root is AMAN, essentially meaning "truly." The transliterations of many words we see such as AMEIN or OMEIN are simply people following one another who are all trying to avoid "AMEN" because someone scared them about it many decades ago. If we do research and test what we are taught, we can avoid being in the dark about such things. The Truth is clean, and there is no darkness associated with it. Adding vowels to avoid foreign word associations is silly when you think about it, but getting to the root word in Hebrew and associating it with other related Hebrew words (instead of foreign words) is more appropriate.

www.fossilizedcustoms.com/blessings.html

BLESSED

The Hebrew word BARUK (H1263, BETH-RESH-UAU-KAF) means delightful, joyful, favorable, blissful, and happy. Some are afraid to use the word "HAPPY" because they have been told it is the proper noun for an Egyptian deity, **HAPI**. Even the Hebrew words **BAAL** (lord, owner), **ADON** (sovereign), and **AL** (strong one) have been called into question, but these only become problematic if used to refer to pagan deities – as names – not clean, useful pronouns.

The etymology for bliss is Old Saxon, BLIZZA.

The word BLIZZA informs the later Old English word BLOD, as the sound of the letter combination DZ evolved to the ending D. BLOD is the etymology of the English word BLOOD.

Many are very concerned that "BLESS" is a tainted word because it is associated with the word BLOD. Pagans use the same word, so this automatically means it must be completely avoided, right? No, it only applies to foreign deities' names.

This word BLESS is not a pagan deity's name, but a word **used by pagans**. Exodus / Shemoth 23:13 orders us to never take the **names** of foreign alahim on our **lips**. It does not tell us to avoid the language – written or spoken - of unbelievers, pagans, scoundrels, idolaters, or people named "George" based on the fact it's Greek for "earth-worker."

If we don't want to use the word BLESS because it is used by pagans, then taking the reasoning to its logical conclusion we would have to also avoid the use of the word BLOOD. Pagans may use thousands of words to communicate, and some of them for their ritual expressions, such as kill, sacrifice, giving, offering, Sun, Moon, or the word "drink."

Psalm 1 begins with the word ASHER, meaning happy, blessed, joyful, blissful. If we use the word BLESSED as a translation, there is no blood expressed in the **meaning**. When a word is used, the **context** it is used in informs how we apply **meaning** to it. It doesn't mean we apply every meaning a word may have listed in the dictionary; we have to **discern** the meaning from the context in which the word is used.

At Malaki 4:2, we see translations such as the KJV or NIV read: "the Sun of righteousness," as the Hebrew word SHAMASH (H8121) can mean "Sun." Primarily the word means SERVANT, and the Sun is "called" SHAMASH because it is a servant. Pagans later worshipped the Sun, and named it SHAMMASH. The phrase at Malaki 4:2 should be translated: "Servant of righteousness" because the Sun is not what the context is referring to.

In the same way, the meaning of a word like BLESS is based upon how it is used in the specific context. If we apply all possible meanings to every word we use, confusion will increase dramatically. Where a word is from is not the problem. The problem is our attitude about where the word is from.

"But keep away from foolish questions, and genealogies, and strife and quarrels about the Torah, for they are unprofitable and useless." – Titus 3:9 (See also 1Tim 6:4 & 2Tim 2:14)

MARK OF THE BEAST - Interpreted By Wisdom Only
The prophecy at Revelation 13 is a riddle concerning a behavior: buying and selling. Christianity never solved the riddle because they were kept from understanding how buying and selling could be involved in the mark of the beast. They are more interested in barcodes being the mark, thinking the barcodes have to be avoided. We don't buy and sell on Yahuah's Shabath.
What needs to be avoided is something so simple they don't believe it when we tell them. The sign of the Eternal Covenant eludes them, and they lack the Key of Knowledge.
The Word, the Name, are above all (Ps. 138:2).
http://www.fossilizedcustoms.com/mark.html

Trinity Wormwood: - the essential doctrine of Catholicism according to Athanasius, the "Father of Orthodoxy."
We can trust Scripture, but traditions never. Adding to what the Word teaches is forbidden. To find trinities, we have to go outside Scripture and sound doctrine, and we find they are everywhere. **The original trinity is Nimrod, Semiramis, and Tammuz** (Nimrod reincarnated). This downloaded into Hinduism's **Brahma, Vishnu, and Shiva.** The list goes on and on, and mixed into the founding doctrines under Constantine's Council at Nicea, based on Alexandrian fathers' baptismal creeds previously established.
http://www.fossilizedcustoms.com/trinity.html

WE STUMBLE OVER WORDS
Head, heart, lamp, wineskin, mind, . . . these all refer abstractly to our thoughts, and from what is in our thoughts comes forth behavior based on our motives derived from our mind. Yahusha searches "minds and hearts" - this is the Hebrew way of expressing the same thing in two ways as a means of reiterating the idea for the sake of emphasis.
We often stumble for the true meaning because:

1. A translator may have missed an idiomatic expression of a word or phrase and taken it literally, thus inserting a **concrete** concept for something intended to be **abstract**; or
2. A translator dismisses the context (surrounding texts) and expresses a word as it appears in other places, where it has other meanings based on the context elsewhere.

THE END IS NEAR

Reapers are standing by to end all rebellion, and a new reign is coming. Envoys are appearing everywhere, and they are called Natsarim. (Google it)
The false teaching authorities of men are all leaven (corruption). We identify the followers who walk in Truth by two main things: They obey the Commandments of Yahuah, and hold to the Testimony of Yahusha (see Rev. 12 & 14).
We test or determine who is in Yahusha's body by their behavior and words, which is the fruit of His Presence in their lives.
We have to sow the seeds (Ten Commandments) that will eventually **produce the fruit**. Some try to lecture about the fruit but avoid sowing the seeds. **What is sown is what grows.**
The weed seed are the rules of men, which if we analyse carefully is only fruit, not seed. The goal is love (fruit), but we have to sow the seeds that produce love (Ten Commandments). The message of the reign is:
"Repent, the reign of Yahuah draws near." Repent, or perish.
We repent by **obeying** the will of Yahuah. The message of AliYahu is to **remember the Torah of Mosheh.**
That final warning is found at Malaki 4:1-6.
http://www.fossilizedcustoms.com/reapers.html

TORAH IS TRUTH – YAHUAH'S GOOD SEED

Sow the good Seeds of the kingdom, and they will bear good fruit in their season. If we guard the Commandments, we will bear their fruit. All who hate Torah (wisdom) love death. Constantine's Christianity threw out the Seeds, and sowed weed seed (men's traditions). Wormwood is the bitter fruit we see choking the life out of the world today.
When we change Yahuah's Words, we feed on wormwood.
http://www.fossilizedcustoms.com/constantine.htm

WITCHCRAFT HAS BEEN INSTITUTIONALIZED

This hidden witchcraft (rebellion) is known by the Greek designation: *Christianity*.

The proof of this rebellion will awaken millions.

The best place to hide witchcraft has been in plain sight.

If you hear the Ten Commandments, and they sound unachievable for you, **you have been taught this by men**, not Yahuah. Wormwood is also a mindset (or spirit) of bitterness: a harsh, sour attitude toward the idea of obeying Yahuah's Commands. You can sense the **bitter spirit** in those who speak against guarding the Commandments. To those filled with this wormwood, people who want to obey are heretics (they use the word "legalists").

A ROOT OF BITTERNESS - WORMWOOD

Yahuah's Torah is despised, and believed to have been "done away" or "nailed to the crux." Some even teach it was only given to prove to us we couldn't obey, and have now been taken away by being nailed to the tree. This is a false teaching: wormwood.

The Commandments were not nailed to the tree. The thing nailed to the tree was the **list of our crimes**. Yahusha became crime (sin) for us, and He was nailed to the stake for our transgressions, and He suffered the penalty we legally deserved: **DEATH**. He substituted His own life for ours. We'll see His scars when we meet Him for the first time, and the sight of them will be overwhelming to each one of us. We will bow in joyful worship.

This **list** of our crimes, called by the term **chierographon**, or *hand-writing*, is a **legal term**. It is a **list of accusations** that were **"against us"** but has been taken out of the hand of our accuser. This false interpretation and alteration of Scripture has caused a **root of bitterness** to grow in peoples' attitude toward the Ten Commandments, rather than <u>sin</u>.

It would be far better to have a **root of bitterness** toward *sin*, since that would be something we would have in common with Yahuah! To them, Yahuah's Torah is the wormwood!

Kolossians 2:14 has been used by our enemy to deceive us, and caused us to feed on this bitterness, **wormwood**.

The **chierographon** lists our sin-debt; it is not the Torah of Yahuah. Due to false teachings of the <u>fathers</u> (Catechetical School of Alexandria), we **"have inherited only falsehood, futility, and there is no value in them."** - YirmeYahu 16:19

This is how the *BYNV* translates the Truth of Kolossians 2:14:
"having blotted-out the certificate-of-debt* against us – by the dogmas – which stood against us. And He has taken it out of the way, having nailed it to the stake." *cheirographon
This **certificate-of-debt** is the chierographon, meaning a hand-written list of accusations. It is a term used in a court of law.
It is the list documenting the crimes of a defendant. The enemy cannot prosecute us, we have been redeemed by the blood of Yahusha. Cheirographon literally means *hand-writing*.
Yahuah's **Torah** is not *hand-writing*, but it is the **everlasting Covenant** He has declared will endure as long as Heaven and Earth endure (see YirmeYahu 31:36, 37, and Mt. 5:18).

ORDAINED BY WHOM? (see 1 Korinthians 1:10, Jer./YirmeYahu 23:21-32)
  Christians are taught by men *ordained* by their denominations. The denominations are variations of Christianity as taught by former elders, and according to their opinions. Ordination means someone is given *orders*, or an appointment to teach according to a specific teaching authority's **line of instruction** (yoke).
It grants a person *permission to teach* within the orderly pattern of their sect. The one they ordain is bound and obligated to defend their method of teaching within strict boundaries.
Many sects forbid their adherents to read outside materials or associate with other denominations.
In their training they closely study the writings of men called *church fathers* who were headmasters at the Catechetical School of Alexandria (CSA). It is also known as the Didascalia, and de l'Ecole d'Alexandrie. This school was founded about 190 CE by **Pantaenus**, although Eusebius (one of the headmasters in the 4th century) claims it was founded by Mark.
This is quite impossible, since this school despised the Natsarim, the followers of Yahusha, labelling them heretics for guarding the Commandments as written, and for possessing Hebrew writings.
One of their headmasters, Epiphanius, described the Natsarim as possessing the writings of MatithYahu in Hebrew lettering as it was originally written.
Pastors today insist the first followers wrote everything in Greek.
The revising of history is nothing new.

Revising (altering) *anything* is a kind of wormwood, since the motive for doing so would have to be because the Truth is a bitter pill to swallow for those who hold tightly to men's traditions. **Exposure to the Truth (the Light) is abhorrent to interlopers posing as messengers of Light.**
What is the end of the entire matter?
 "Let us hear the conclusion of the entire matter:
Fear Alahim and guard His Commands, for this *applies* to all mankind! For Alahim shall bring every work into right-ruling, including all that is hidden, whether good or evil."
Eccl. 12:13, 14
If you learn a custom or ritual originates from pagan behavior, stay away from it. Walk as Yahusha walked, and stay in His will at all times. He is always beside you to call on for help and strength to discern.
You will hear His Spirit say, *"This is the Way, walk in it."*

WORMWOOD IS AS WORMWOOD DOES
There's no sign or indication we worship Yahuah if all we do is recycle pagan trash (middens), and ignore obeying the simple things He ordered us to do to show we love Him.
Where in Scripture to we find Yahuah is offended by "legalism?"
We are in Yahusha, and Yahusha is in us.
I am my Beloved's, and my Beloved is mine. Song of Shalomoh 6:3
Yahusha's peace releases us from so much anxiety about what might happen in the future. He's coming back home, and His **wife** is His home. The more we listen to interpretations of prophecies, the more we realize the prophecies will matter most when they are fulfilled, not before. There are so many anxious about the "four blood moons" or what this and that might portend, but throughout Scripture Yahuah pleads, with those who will hear, to return to the Covenant. If we, His Natsarim, also keep repeating the same message over and over, it's only because Yahuah is making us do so. When you can say your fear is not valid anymore, and you feel peace about what is coming, you know the love of Yahusha from your heart.
There is a chemistry at work between those who love Yahusha enough to step out of the herd and obey Him in love.
His sweetness is in us, but we smell like death to all others.

The flashing sword of love (His Word) is in our hearts.

**"So Yahusha said to those Yahudim who believed Him,
'If you stay in My Word, you are truly My taught ones, and
you shall know the truth, and the truth shall make you free.'"**
- Yn. 8:31-32

The changing of the Torah by Constantine (prophesied at Dan. 7:25)
does not change it, it is **an attempt** to change it. The 7th day of
the week was blessed, and set-apart by Yahuah, so we see in
the Millennial reign **"from Shabath to Shabath"** all flesh will
bow to Him. This will not be the Day of the Sun each week.
Yahusha told us in the last days to **"pray your flight will not be
in winter, or on the Shabath."**
Heaven and Earth are still here, and until these both pass away,
we must stand only on the foundation laid by Yahusha, since we
are to **"walk even as He walked."** Constantine said, "let us
have nothing in common with the hostile rabble of the Yahudim."
Since it seems the Natsarim "live in Old Testament times" in
contrast to those who follow Constantine and the circus fathers'
allegorical interpretations, how can we dismiss Is. 8:20, and this
clear statement from 1 Yn. 2:4-7:
**"The one who says, 'I know Him,' and does not guard His
commands, is a liar, and the Truth is not in him. But
whoever guards His Word, truly the love of Alahim has been
perfected in him. By this we know that we are in Him.
The one who says he stays in Him ought himself also to
walk, even as He walked. Beloved, I write no fresh command
to you, but an old Command which you have had from the
beginning. The old Command is the Word which you heard
from the beginning."**
The "old Command is the **Word** which you heard from the
beginning" was altered in 321 CE by Constantine with the first
"Sun-day law." (See book *Sunday Origins* by this author).

CONSTANTINE'S CREED
"I renounce all customs, rites, legalisms, unleavened breads and
sacrifices of lambs of the Hebrews, and all the other feasts of the
Hebrews, sacrifices, prayers, aspirations, purifications,
sanctifications, and propitiations, and fasts and new moons, and
Sabbaths, and superstitions, and hymns and chants, and
observances and synagogues. absolutely everything Jewish,

every Law, rite and custom and if afterwards I shall wish to deny and return to Jewish superstition, or shall be found eating with Jews, or feasting with them, or secretly conversing and condemning the Christian religion instead of openly confuting them and condemning their vain faith, then let the trembling of Cain and the leprosy of Gehazi cleave to me, as well as the legal punishments to which I acknowledge myself liable. And may I be an anathema in the world to come, and may my soul be set down with satan and the devils."

(Stefano Assemani, Acta Sanctorium Martyrum Orientalium at Occidentalium, Vol. 1, Rome 1748, page 105) **Antiochus Epiphanes viewed himself as Zeus manifest:**

ANTIOCHUS EPIPHANES – 165 BCE (Epiphanes means manifest)

This Greek ruler set up an image of Zeus in the Temple, a type of the abomination of desolation spoken of in Danial 11.
His desecrations and cruelty persisted for over 3 years.
He established these laws over the Yahudim:

You shall profane the Sabbath
You shall change the set times (festivals) and laws
You shall set up idols
You shall eat unclean animals
You shall not circumcise
You shall forget Torah

3 years and 2 months later, the Temple was taken back and rededicated. This is known as the Feast of Dedication, or Festival of Lights. The Hebrew word Hanukkah means dedication. This festival became a civil celebration, and is mentioned at Yahukanon / John 10:22.

WERE YOU TAUGHT THERE ARE SACRAMENTS?

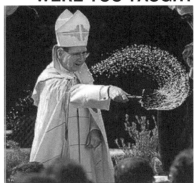 

When the Star Trek crew pretends the cardboard fixtures they fiddle with are real, operational weapons, tractor beams, or transporters, those watching also pretend they are real. It's a fantasy, but while it is happening everyone pretends it is real. Religion is the same imaginary pretense. Reality is where we need to be, so we will become sober. We need de-programming. In Latin, the words *hoc es corpus meum* literally mean "this is My body." These words spoken originally in Hebrew by Yahusha *were pointing to Himself, and His body of followers.* <u>We</u> are His body, and He is the Head of His body.

The "unleavened" aspect represented that body (1 Cor 5:7), uncorrupted by the teachings of men. The *teachings of men* are referred to in Scripture as *leaven*.

He is the Head; and we His body partake of His sufferings. Instead of Passover, the Circus calls the repeated ritual of remembering Yahusha's death *"the sacrifice of the Mass"* and a *"bloodless sacrifice."* In this ritual, it was believed the common bread **transubstantiates** into the *living body* of Yahusha. This concept caused even more idolatry, such as genuflecting to the *"Host."* It encourages literal worship and prayer to a displayed "Host" in an object called a monstrance. *This violates the first, second, and third Commandments.*

These teachings are abominations in the cup of Circe (a name for the woman, aka Babel), causing the world to become drunken (mad), and such idolatry keeps the world unclean before the Throne of Yahuah, incurring His blazing wrath on the Day of Yahuah:

"Flee from the midst of Babel, and let each one save his life! Do not be cut off in her crookedness, for this is the time of the vengeance of Yahuah, the recompense He is repaying her. Babel was a golden cup in the hand of Yahuah, making

drunk all the Earth. The nations drank her wine, that is why the nations went mad!" - Jer / YirmeYahu 51:6, 7 (see also 2 Pet 3, ZekarYah 14, Malaki 4, 1 Thess 5,2 Thess 1, Mt 24, Yual [Joel] 2)

Worship of the Host in a sunburst monstrance is idolatry:

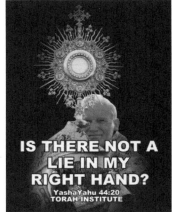

The worship of the "host of heaven" (Acts 7:42) involved the zodiac; the sun, moon, and stars, and one of the elements was the image of the crux, which depicted the *equinoxes*, the intersection of the celestial meridian and the celestial equator twice each year.

REPAIRERS OF THE BREACH

The Ten Commandments are the "eternal" Covenant, and they teach us how to love Yahuah, and love our neighbor - they are not difficult, they are our great commission to teach, the "old paths" in which to dwell. Natsarim are the repairers of the breach before the reapers come on the Day of Yahuah. The 7th day of each week is also called **"the set-apart Day of Yahuah."**
Isa / YashaYahu 58:12-14:

"And those from among you shall build the old waste places. You shall raise up the foundations of many generations. And you would be called the Repairer of the Breach, the Restorer of Streets to Dwell In.
If you do turn back your foot from the Shabath, from doing your pleasure on My set-apart day, and shall call the Shabath 'a delight,' the set-apart day of Yahuah 'esteemed,' and shall esteem it, not doing your own ways, nor finding your own pleasure, nor speaking your own words, then you shall delight yourself in Yahuah. And I shall cause you to ride on the heights of the earth, and feed you with the

inheritance of YaAqob your father. For the mouth of Yahuah has spoken!"

Paul's writings are misunderstood by the lawless, as Peter explained at 3 Pet. 3:16. Paul explains at Kolossians 2 how the **"shadows of things to come for the body of Yahusha"** outline our **redemption**. Yahusha has sealed us with His Name for the **day of our redemption**, which is one of those shadows: **Yom Kafar**, when reapers are unleashed to harvest the Earth (see book, *REAPERS*). Most will be burned, but the first-fruits will be protected by the same seraphim doing the reaping. The weeds are removed first; afterward the wheat is gathered into the New Yerushalayim.

The redemptive shadows were rejected by Constantine since the whole culture of Torah was abhorred by his direct order.

The interpretation of Paul by the lawless circus fathers was revealed by Paul himself at Acts 20 when he spoke with the elder Natsarim of his own time. He said men would arise from them who were savage wolves, not sparing the flock. When the Light dawns on you, you will see Psalm 1 and Psalm 119 as being the pure thoughts of Yahuah's plan for all mankind. (see also Eccl. 12:13, Rev. 12, Rev. 14). Anyone who annuls the least of the Commandments will be the least in the reign of Yahusha, but *he who guards and teaches them* will be the greatest.

LEGALISM or ILLEGALISM?

Being "legal" is thought of as heretical to today's religious leadership. Usually the term "legalist" is a way of dismissing those who seek to obey the will of Yahuah as it is written.

The term "legalist" is used as a synonym for "heretic." Obedience proves our faith, and when our faith is perfected in such a way that we are being "legal" in Yahuah's eyes, He knows by our active obedience that we love Him. One cannot prove their commitment to Yahuah by being illegal, and having no plan to become legal, and show improvement in that direction. 2 Peter 1 advises us to *increase* in our uprightness, and thereby do our utmost in making firm our calling.

The Pharisees were fakers, and obeyed the traditions of men rather than seek to obey Yahuah from their hearts.

Yahusha was never upset at them for being legal and **obeying Torah**, but rather for substituting the **traditions of men** in place

of obeying Yahuah - *exactly where we find ourselves today with the illegalists in Christian leadership.*
Church tradition, not Torah, is their focus.
They want our tithe, but they don't teach the righteousness of Yahuah, His Ten Commandments.
We are ambassadors of the coming reign of Yahusha, and very much seek to be the greatest legalists of all as we purify our walk and wait for the coming of our Master. We're ironing the wrinkles out of our wedding garments, and trimming our lamps with the extra oil He is pouring into our hearts - the wisdom of the five wise virgins is knowing what is pleasing to Him.
We beg, be restored to favor with Yahuah; He is coming sooner than you expect.

THE FUSION OF PAGAN CULTURES AT ALEXANDRIA
XPISTIANOS Found 3 times in the Received Text (NT)
The term **Christian** was used by the Greek culture several hundred years before Yahusha's birth in Bethlehem.
Rome (Italy) and Alexandria (Egypt) were the western world's primary repositories of knowledge.
A merger of ancient Egyptian, Greek, and Roman cultures took place from 300 BCE to 200 CE, and Christianity emerged from it.
The Greek deity **Serapis** replaced Osiris as the consort of Isis, and the devotees of this deity were called "**Christians**."
Hadrian (Roman emperor 117 to 138) built the **Pantheon** (temple to all gods) using concrete to form the world's largest domed structure (domes are a pagan design from Hinduism's Shivalingam design).
He wrote that **Serapis** and **IESU** were the *same deity*.
This is syncretism, and when it catches on, it becomes tradition. **People serve traditions with ferocious zeal.**
Confusion and syncretism between pagan cultures at Rome and Alexandria continued into the 4th century CE.
The Alexandrian cult, or **church fathers**, worked feverishly to synthesize paganism with the Messianic movement, hatching their brand under the Serapis' followers' name, **Christians**, who occupied the city for centuries before them.
The followers of Yahusha were called **Natsarim** (branches, watchmen, guardians – see Acts 24:5). We guard (shamar) the Name and the Word. To the Greeks, the impaled Mashiak is foolishness (1 Cor. 1:23), so the Greek term "xpristianos"

(meaning *idiot*) seemed appropriate to them. The Greek term CHRISTIANOS in that day was a term foisted on them, causing **suffering** as Peter writes about it at 1 Peter 4:15-16.

No one would ever want to be labeled a murderer, thief, doer of evil, or meddler. Nor would they wish to be known as an idiot or *"cretin."* The words **christ** and **christian** are unrelated.

Look at the **context** of this rarely-used term, **christianos***:*

"For do not let any of you suffer as a murderer, or thief, or doer of evil, or as a meddler. But if (*one suffers*) **as a xpistianos, let him not be ashamed, but let him esteem Alahim in this matter."** – 1 Peter 4:15-16

The word was used as a pronoun to denigrate and shame the Natsarim. It was a term of contempt and scorn. If you look up the origin of the word **cretin**, you'll see the Greek source is xpistianos. Tradition revised it.

We should never **call one another** such a term. It means *an idiot,* but revisionism has caused mass-amnesia.

Please Google the term CRETIN, and learn the truth.

I ASKED THE MAGISTERIUM A QUESTION

The following question was asked from the AskACatholic web site on Saturday, August 15, 2015:

"Yahusha's teaching authority was questioned by the chief priests and elders at Mt. 21:23. They, like the existing Magisterium, had set up their own authority, above Scripture. What is the name of the one you worship?

And, if you claim it is Yahuah, what example of obedience to Him can you offer as a sign of that worship?

As Christianity evolved over many centuries, many alterations occurred such that resting from work on the Sabbath became transferred to the first day, abstaining from unclean animals was no longer required. As there are no examples given from Scripture of these and many other practices now adopted, it has been said that "Church tradition" retains authority to do the very same things that incurred Yahusha's wrath about the Sanhedrin in His day. In this context, praying to dead people (necromancy and divination) would seem to be another example of such church tradition.

If Yahuah does not change, and such things are an abomination to Him, by what authority do you do these things, and by what name do you call on for deliverance?" - Lew White

AskACatholic responded by sharing links to pages with prepared answers. One mentioned how the Catholics wrote the Bible, for Catholics, for use in the Church. My simple questions went unanswered, and I still didn't know who they claim to worship. My reply to them follows:

The Roman Catholic dogmas don't reveal who is being worshipped.

If I obey the 4th Commandment to rest on the 7th day, I'm a heretic (according to the Council of Laodicea, 365 CE).

Catholics did not write or give us Scripture.

The first followers of Yahusha were not Catholics. Yahusha is not a Catholic. The assembly is not an institution, but a body controlled by Yahusha, the Head. The dogmas of Catholicism reveal a very different pattern of behavior than Yahusha's walk:

ROMAN CHURCH TIMELINE OF WORMWOOD
(from the Catholic Encyclopedia)
DATE / DOGMA

CE 300 Full immersion changed to affusion (sprinkle).

CE 300 Prayers to the dead. NECROMANCY, a form of divination (Against Dt. 18:11 & YashaYahu 8:19)

CE 310 Making the "sign" of the CROSS.

CE 325 Anathema (death) decreed to anyone who adds or changes the creed of faith of Nice. (See years 1545 & 1560). EASTER was established at Nicea.

CE 365-370 Council of Laodicea rejects Apocrypha, calls Shabath observers "Judaizers", worthy of death. This council refers to "Shabath" as distinct from the *LORD's Day* (Baal's Day).

CE 375 Veneration of angels and dead saints (Veneration means worship)

CE 394 Institution of the **Sacrament of the Mass**:
Missa Recitata, Low Mass, priest + 1
Missa Cantata, Sung Mass, priest + 1
Missa Solemnis, High Mass, priest + 2
Missa Pontificalis, Bishop + priest + ?

CE 431 The worship of Miryam (Mary) [veneration is worship]

CE 431 Miryam "Queen of Heaven" (against YirmeYahu 7:18, 44:17, 44:25)

CE 431 Miryam "ever virgin" (against Mt. 1:25, Mk. 6:3, Yn. 2:2-4).

CE 431 Miryam "Mediatrix" (against 1 Tim. 2:5, Yn. 11:28).

CE 500 Priestcraft began to dress in "priestly garb".

CE 526 Sacrament of "Extreme Unction"

CE 593 Doctrine of "Purgatory" (Yn. 5:24, 1Yn. 1:7-9, 2:1,2, Romans 8:1)

CE 600 Latin language only language permitted for prayer (1 Cor. 14:9)

CE 709 Kissing the feet of pope is ordered (Acts 10:25,26, Rev. 19:10, 22:8,9)

CE 750 Temporal Power of pope declared (Mt. 4:8,9, 20:25,26, Yn. 18:38)

CE 754 Council of Constantinople ordered removal of all images and abolition of image worship.

CE 785 Miryam "co-redemptrix" (Acts 4:12, Ps. 146:5, Hebrews 7:25)

CE 788 Miryam "worship" (against Romans 1:25, Yasha Yahu 42:8, Mk. 3:21)

CE 788 Worship of cross, relics, and images re-authorized (against Ex. 20:4, Dt. 12:3, 27:15, Ps. 115:4-8)

CE 850 Fabrication and use of "holy water" (adopted from Hinduism's sacred water of the Ganges River)

CE 890 Veneration of St. Yosef, husband of Miryam. (see CE 788 listings)

CE 965 Baptism of the bells ~ ceremony of "baptizing" bells to ward off demons and to call the elect to vespers when blessed bells are rung.

CE 995 Canonization of dead saints (against Romans 1:7, 1 Cor. 1:2)

CE 998 Fasting on "Fri-days" & during "Lent" (against Mt. 15:11, 1 Cor. 10:25, 1 Tim. 4:1-8)

CE 1079 Celibacy of priestcraft declared (married priests ordered to cast-off wives, against 1 Tim. 3:2-5, 3:12, Mt. 8:14,15).

CE 1090 Institution of rosary prayer beads, or *chaplet* (against Mt. 6:7, Dt. 18:10,11 YashaYahu 8:19 ~ also, Buddhism, Shinto, and Islam practice prayer-bead counting)

CE 1190 Sale of indulgences (against Eph. 2:8-10). For those of you who don't know, this was a practice of people paying the clergy to have punishment time taken off from burning in "Purgatory" after their death. Eating meat on Friday is a "mortal" sin, so you can't buy an indulgence for doing that – it's straight to hell for you.

CE 1215 Dogma of Transubstantiation declared (against Luke 22:19,20, Mk. 13:21, Yn. 6:35, Mt. 24:23-28, 1 Cor. 11:26) Many were burned at the stake over this false teaching.

CE 1215 Confession of sins to priest ordered (against Ps. 51:1-10, Luke 7:48 & 15:21, 1 Yn. 1:8,9)

CE 1220 Adoration of the wafer host (matsah worship! Against Ex. 20:4, Yn. 4:24)

CE 1229 Scriptures forbidden to laymen (against Yn. 5:39, 8:31, 2 Tim. 3:15-17)

CE 1265 Miryam's house moved by angel to Lorento Italy. (as fishy as this smells, I don't think they violated Torah, unless they were lying ~ what do you think?)

CE 1287 Scapular protection decreed (brown cloth talisman with picture of virgin packed with tea leaves proclaimed to contain supernatural powers or "virtues" to protect wearer

CE 1414 "Chalice" forbidden to laity at "communion" (a radical distortion of the Passover Seder, the annual remembrance of Yahusha's death)

CE 1439 Dogma of seven sacraments (against Mt. 28:19,20, & 26:26-28)

CE 1439 Purgatory declared valid dogma (against Mt. 25:46, Luke 23:43)

CE 1508 Miryam "Mother of GOD" (against Mt. 12:46-50, Lk. 8:19-21, Acts 1:14)

CE 1545 Church tradition equal and able to alter Scripture (against Mt. 15:6, Mk. 7:7-13, Col. 2:8 ~ also adds many other dogma to Council of Nice)

CE 1560 Creed of pope Pius IV decreed (against Gal. 1:8)

CE 1580 Pope declared to be *LORD GOD* (that's enough to get some people roasted. Yahuah will not allow His esteem to go to another YashaYahu 48:11)

CE 1593 *Ave Maria* adopted (means *hail Miryam*)

CE 1710 Stuffed donkey in Verona, Italy, at Church of the Madonna of the Organs, decreed to be the actual animal Yahusha ha Mashiak entered Yerushaliyim on. Visiting it will gain indulgences. Circus animals for the circus!

[When I first heard about this, I couldn't stop laughing for 10 minutes]

CE 1854 Immaculate Conception of Virgin Miryam (against Romans 3:23, & 5:12, Ps. 51:5, YirmeYahu 17:9)

CE 1864 Miryam "sinless" (against Luke 1:46, 47, Romans 3:10-19, & 23).

CE 1870 Papal infallability decreed (against 2 Thess. 2:2-12, Rev. 17:1-9, 13:5-8, 18)

CE 1907 All sciences condemned. (Science is the search for Truth, and the word comes from the Latin word, scio, *to know*)

CE 1922 Pope declared to be "Jesus Christ"

CE 1930 All public schools condemned.

CE 1950 Declaration of the bodily assumption of the Virgin Miryam into Heaven

CE 2008 The Name "Yahweh" forbidden in liturgy, singing, or worship.

CE 2014 Following Pope Francis on Twitter gains indulgences.

If the above isn't wormwood, it will do until the real wormwood comes along, don't you think?

Here is the next reply from AskACatholic's website:
"Catholic or Roman Catholics worship Jesus Christ and ONLY Jesus Christ. Jesus founded ONE Church on St. Peter (Matthew 16:17-19) and said the gates of Hell would not prevail against the Church HE FOUNDED on St. Peter.
Your Date / Dogma list is a complete distortion of what we believe. The only reason this list makes sense to you is because, like all other Protestants, you reject Oral Tradition that has been passed down by word of mouth from pope to pope, bishop to bishop, and priest to priest. The first followers of Jesus were *Catholic Christians*.
. . . please don't distort what we believe as Catholics. If you are unsure what we believe, ask us, not Andy anti-Catholic."

They ignored my points, and claimed the date / dogma list is a complete distortion of what they believe, yet the list of dogmas and dates came from their own *Catholic Encyclopedia!*
My reply: Thanks again for replying with more information this second time. The simple answer of who you worship is very important to anyone, as you can well imagine.

I'm asking a Catholic, not an anti-Catholic, and I hope the whole team will get involved to provide a straight, simple answer to the two simple questions:

1. Who do you worship (obey).
2. What do you practice that proves that you worship (obey) who you say you do.

To a Catholic, the Catholic dogmas matter, since they are "dogmatic" and unalterable even by later dogmas.
I only presented them because they greatly add and take away from the Word of Yahuah, and emphasize obeying (worshipping) traditions of men.
We are to "live by every Word that proceeds from the mouth of Yahuah," not by men's words or traditions.
Traditions, rather than living according to Torah, was the big problem Yahusha had with the Pharisees, Sadducees, and the whole Sanhedrin.
There is no oral tradition recognized by Scripture (including the Talmud), only the unalterable written Word of Yahuah, or "Living Words," as stated at Acts 7:38.
The list of dogmas are from the Catholic encyclopedia, and are a timeline of required <u>Catholic</u> beliefs.
If any Catholic refuses to belief any one of them, they face excommunication by the terms of that faith group (not mine).
If you worship a deity, Jesus, what proof is there in how you live from what He said to do and obey?
We are to walk as He walked (live as He lived).
No doubt you know there was no one named "Jesus" in the first century, and you mean Yahusha (the only Name given).
The IESV, IHS, IES, IC-XC, and IESOUS Greco-Latin christograms and theonyms were devices to conceal the true Name, not reveal it.
If you worship Him, then everything He ordered must be obeyed.
He said to "pray your flight is not in winter, or on the Shabath."
He did not mean the day of the Sun; Constantine altered the day of rest, and Laodicea outlawed resting on the 7th day.
If all the popes, bishops, and priests agreed on error, Yahusha's Word trumps them all. Their words will pass away,
but Yahusha's Words will never pass away.

We are to *"live by every Word that proceeds from the mouth of Yahuah,"* not by men's words or traditions.

In reality, from everything you've said so far, **you worship tradition**, not the Creator, Yahusha. Perhaps I was misunderstood.

What is it that Catholics do that proves they worship Yahusha? No one knew anyone named Jesus until the 17th century on planet Earth.

Please explain where Yahusha told us to get busy with ideas like Purgatory, eternal suffering in fire, relic kissing (veneration of human remains), transubstantiation (bread wafer transforms into living body and blood of Yahusha with words "hoc est corpus meum"), statue veneration (kneeling before objects), steeples/sun pillars, bells, worship of the "host" (in a monstrance – sun burst object), prayers to the dead (necromancy via rosaries), monks, nuns, popes, priests, celibacy, indulgences, trinity doctrine, infant baptism, apostolic succession, sacraments, crosses (symbol of Sun deity everywhere throughout history), replacement of Name Yahuah to "LORD" (Baal), adoption of Easter / Ishtar fertility festival with sunrise worship & egg/bunny/fish symbols, Natalis Sol Invictus (Saturnalia) transformed into "Christ-Mass," a celebration Yahusha's birth, - and much more.

HEBREW ROOTS ARE FEARED

Natsarim are feared by Christian leadership because we obey. Deep down, the Christian teachers know that *all their traditions will not survive the Second Coming,* and they may not either.

The basic difference between the Natsarim and the Christians is not well understood. They adhere to two different things. Christians practice (obey, serve, worship) **tradition**, while being told they "live by every Word that proceeds from the mouth of Yahuah." In fact, they observe nothing Yahuah commanded, and follow the previous traditions of cultures that worshipped the host of heaven (Babel's harlotry, Astrology).

Birthdays, Easter, Christmas, and so many other so-called "secular" practices originate from Babel's witchcraft, now considered cleansed of their former polluted fertility meaning because they are now directed at the worship of "Jesus." This is a *strong delusion*, since men's traditions will not survive the Second Coming.

When Yahusha comes back, the reign of Babel will have been swept away. No one will be saying, *"what's your sign?"* They will never hear *"I having a birthday party, can you come to it?"* There will be no more Christmas, Santa, tree-decorating, wreath-hanging, Easter bunny, colored eggs, Valentines Day hearts with arrows, tooth fairy, Halloween, or any other arrogant nonsense. People won't be doing many things they do now.

The original followers of Yahusha were called Natsarim (Acts 24:5). In the early centuries after Yahusha ascended, alliances developed between various Sun-worshipping consortiums at Alexandria, Egypt. Today we call them **church fathers**, and their teachings form the **Didache**. Their early name was the **Didascalia** (Greek, *teaching authority*), and later the "Catechetical Schola" (Latin, "echo-teaching school"). Responsatorial teaching was a technique developed to quickly train new adherents. The culture embraced all the traditions of paganism, while *leaving out the pattern of living taught and followed by Yahusha and His Natsarim.* The head masters of the Didascalia wrote of the Natsarim, calling them "heretics" because they did not conform to or recognize the teaching authority of the Catechetical School at Alexandria. Epiphanius (a church father) described Natsarim as living by the same customs as the Jews, only they believed in IESV (their name for Yahusha). He described how the Natsarim held a copy of the gospel of MatithYahu in the "Hebrew script" as it was "originally written." Jerome met one of the Natsarim and wrote about them also. Instead of worshipping traditions of men, Natsarim hold to the witness of Yahusha, and obey the Commandments (as written) of Yahuah.

We preserve His Name, and His Word.

The Latin word for **Didascalia** (teaching authority) is **Magisterium**. The Magisterium controls much of what everyone believes, and this is accomplished by slowly **training people what to think from infancy**.

WE'RE TRAINED TO OBEY TRADITION, AND DISOBEY YAHUAH
JUST AS NIMROD INTENDED FROM THE BEGINNING

Here's why the Ten Commandments matter:

"Blessed are those doing His commands, so that the authority shall be theirs unto the tree of life, and to enter through the gates into the city. But outside are the dogs and those who enchant with drugs, and those who whore, and

the murderers, and the idolaters, and all who love and do falsehood." - Rev. 22:14-15 (see Eccl. 12:13)

www.fossilizedcustoms.com/partingways.html

How Did One Faith Become Two Completely Different Ones?
Yahusha makes this statement at Mt. 4:4:
"'It has been written, "Man shall not live by bread alone, but by every word that comes from the mouth of Yahuah."'"
How can Yahusha's words be reconciled with what we've been taught? **People are eating pigs, bowing to images of crosses, fixing Easter egg baskets, putting trees in their homes on December 25th, using steeples to indicate a worship building, dressing-up like Hindu priests and pretending to change bread and wine into Yahusha's body and splashing "holy water" on people, and generally doing all kinds of things without any notion of their pagan origins.**
A restoration is now taking place, as when Noah stood and cried out to those who would perish in the days of the Great Flood.
Yahusha is the Master of the Shabath, but Constantine transferred it, and the council of Laodicea (365/370 CE) declared all those who rested on the Sabbath to be "Judaizers," and "anathema." (anathema: worthy of death).
If Yahusha is **Master of the Shabath**, and Yahuah does not change, is His behavior now **"anathema?"**
Yahusha said His Words would **"never pass away."**
How did we come to practice everything Yahuah told us not to practice (which pagans were doing), and not practice a single thing He told us to practice? While these things are blatantly obvious, why is it that so few seem to be awake enough to notice? What is His Name, and what is His Word?

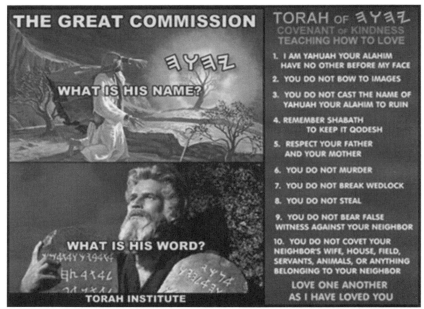

"So Yahusha said to those Yahudim who believed Him, 'If you stay in My Word, you are truly My taught ones, and you shall know the Truth, and the Truth shall make you free.'" - Yn. 8:31-32

SIGN OF THE EVERLASTING COVENANT: CHANGED?

Yahusha stated that He is the Master of Yom Shabath (Luke 6:5). What Day Is Shabath? Speaking of the last days and the great distress at Mt. 24:20, Yahusha told His pupils who would be alive during the Day of Yahuah **"And pray that your flight does not take place in winter or on the Shabath."**

The weekly Shabath is the only day blessed by Yahuah, and He states it is a sign forever between Him and His people "forever." How can men transfer or alter this?

The Catholic dogma is that the resurrection of Yahusha is the basis for the transference of the day of rest to the first day, but that is a deception to remove the sign of the everlasting Covenant, and adopt the sign of Sun-day, Sun worship's special day. Sunday is like GMO fruit; it's man-altered and not eternal. The seed was stolen by the birds (demons who sowed weed-seed). First-fruits (one of the 7 high days) had always been a shadow of redemption, and Yahusha full-filled it by becoming the First-fruits which the wave sheaf offering pointed to.

70

In approximately 365 CE, the Council of Laodicea outlawed Shabath, and pronounced anathema-status on any who obeyed the 4th Commandment: **"Christians must not Judaize by resting on the Sabbath, but must work on that day, rather honoring the Lord's Day; and, if they can, resting then as Christians. But if any shall be found to be Judaizers, let them be anathema from Christ."**

Yahusha's reference at Mt. 24:20 has been falsely interpreted by preterists, but read His Word again from Mt. 24:20-21:

"And pray that your flight does not take place in winter or on the Shabath. For then there shall be great distress, such as has not been since the beginning of the world until this time, no, nor ever shall be."

The Catholic doctrine, followed by Protestants, is in direct conflict on this point, and endangers everyone misled by it.

Constantine's Christianity would in his words, **"have nothing in common with the hostile rabble of the Yahudim."**

They share nothing in common, the wormwood replaced it all. The Circus fathers made sure of this, and today Christians obey the Circus councils rather than have anything in common with Yahusha's walk, or any of His moral teachings or cultural patterns, except tithing.

How easy it would have been if we had only been taught to obey the Torah! The reapers will remove all things offensive, then gather the wheat into the New Yerushalayim at Yahusha's coming. Even if we are united in error, we will perish.

The "Living Word" is the Word we are to "live" in, and any other word is off the path of life, and not walking as Yahusha walked. Most people still don't even know His true and only Name.

"To the Torah and to the witness! If they do not speak according to this Word, it is because they have no light of dawn." - YashaYahu / Isaiah 8:20 BYNV

Proverbs 3 tells us wisdom is Torah, the instructions of Yahuah. Torah is personified as a *she*, and is also referred to as the *Tree of Life*. At Proverbs 8, we glean much more about Torah.

"By me sovereigns reign, and rulers make righteous decrees. By me princes rule, and nobles, all the judges of the earth. I love those who love me, and those who earnestly seek me do find me." - Proverbs 8:15-17 *Do you love the Torah?*

"And now, listen to me, you children, for blessed are they

who guard my ways. Listen to discipline and become wise, and do not refuse it. Blessed is the man who listens to me, watching daily at my gates, waiting at the posts of my doors. For whoever finds me shall find life, and obtain favor from Yahuah, But he who sins against me injures himself. All who hate me love death!" - Pro 8:32-36

The New World Order is the ecumenical utopia of the beast.

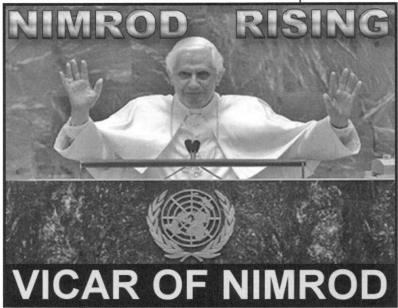

WISDOM & THE MARK OF THE BEAST

Proverbs 1:6 tells us **wisdom *enables us to understand*** proverbs, figures of speech, **and riddles. People who are in the beast don't recognize it. The mark is something they do.**
The *mark of the beast* is a riddle, only solvable by having "wisdom." Wisdom is the knowledge of Torah, simply the Ten Commandments.
Those who follow the **beast** (reign of Babel) don't know which day we are to rest, and not buy and sell. You can figure it out if you have ears to hear (the Word of Yahuah).
The beast's **mark** is the ancient symbol and weekly conduct seen openly everywhere. The ancient Sun worshipers assembled on the Day of the Sun (Sun-day), in the morning, with a pillar (steeple), rang bells, and honored the symbol of the sun, the crux. These customs are not from Yahuah's Word,

but from Nimrod's worship of the host of heaven - witchcraft. Yahuah's mark? The seventh day, which He blessed at creation. What are we to do? Stop and rest. Obedience is worship. We are servants of the one we obey (Romans 6:16).

RELIGION OF TRADITIONS

The Second Coming will wipe-clean the traditions and decisions of all the councils, and we will reboot to the Living Words of Yahuah only. Natsarim don't use any sacraments, and our fellowship with Yahusha as our only Head and teaching authority is vastly different from the fourth beast's religion of traditions.

We simply teach the Commandments as written, and they shape hearts with Yahuah's will, and love is the outcome. Yahusha is in charge at all times, and no one gets burned, hung, or even judged. We work among those who serve their religious traditions, but we don't observe those traditions.

We are free, because we live in Yahuah's Word, not men's traditions. You can wrestle with what men think, but the yoke (teachings) of Yahusha will set you free.

Religion is tradition; but knowing the will of Yahusha is reality, and produces the fruits of His Spirit. Arius was right, and persecuted by the Alexandrian Cult, but Natsarim don't argue about such things. The words of Athanasius will pass away, but the Word of Yahuah will remain forever.

Natsarim reflect Yahusha's teachings by **"living by every Word that proceeds from the mouth of Yahuah,"** and we surrender in humility to living by His instructions. We shed the heavy yoke of men's teachings.

If you want to stand before the Throne of the universe and explain your preference to live by a "non-legal" method, that's always a choice to be made. We are already non-legal, but moving in the direction of the Living Words (to live by) is not heretical or evil. We are ambassadors, as if Yahuah Himself is pleading with people to be restored to favor.

If we pleaded with them to just believe and live under "grace" and to ignore the fact they are eating ham, working their job on the day we were told to rest, and calling Yahuah by whatever name tradition has taught us to call Him, we live in a delusion. Yahusha is the Living Word, and we are told to **"walk even as He walked."**

Those who do not live by the Commandments do not know Him, and do not belong to Him. Unintentional sin (crime) is where "grace" applies. To sin intentionally, while knowing what is right but ignoring it, is where grace does not apply. Ask Yahusha how He wants you to live. If you live the way He wants, you will not fit into the religion of tradition, and will be shunned by everyone who wants to remain the way they are.

"Here is the endurance of the set-apart ones; here are those who are guarding the Commandments of Alahim _and_ the belief of Yahusha." – Rev. 14:12

Unbelieving Yahudim or Christians cannot claim to be these "first-fruits" described in this verse at Rev 14:12, nor this verse:

"Blessed are those _doing_ His Commands, so that the authority shall be theirs unto the tree of life and to enter through the gates into the city." - Rev 22:14

Scripture doesn't say, "Blessed are those practicing the Talmud." The Talmud did not exist in the days of Yahusha, Paul, Luke, and the rest of the Talmidim (students). It was in the form of the "oral law", the traditions of the elders, and Yahusha nor any of His followers had anything to do with it.

WHAT ABOUT THE ORAL LAW?
There is still a division over what some perceive as traditions "orally" handed-down. Every Word of Yahuah was written, and read aloud to the people. The oral instructions, or **traditions of the fathers,** was the paradigm Paul said was his **former way of** living by. He called it "**Yahudaism,**" (traditions of the fathers).
"For you have heard of my former way of life in Yahudaism, how intensely I persecuted the assembly of Alahim, and ravaged it."
Note the phrase, **"former way of life"** at Gal 1:13.
This "yoke" (teaching authority) of men is described here:
"Now then, why do you try Alahim by putting a yoke on the neck of the taught ones which neither our fathers nor we were able to bear?" - Acts 15:10.
The yoke of the **traditions of the fathers** (the leaven of men's teachings) Yahusha called "old wine." They drank the wormwood. The traditions of men are the object lesson from Matsah (Unleavened Bread). We must become unleavened, purging the teaching authorities and corrupting influences of men's ideas

which block the pure and clean objective of love, which the Torah's goal is to teach us.

THE NATIONS WENT MAD

There's a source, or wellspring from which all the Earth has become drunk. It is personified to be a **woman** who causes all the world to be drunk on the contents of a "golden cup." Revelation calls her the mother of harlots or Babel the Great. YirmeYahu (Jer.) 7 & 44 refer to her as the "**queen of heaven**." Jer/YirmeYahu 51:7: "**Babel was a golden cup in the hand of Yahuah, making drunk all the Earth. The nations drank her wine, that is why the nations went mad!**"

The Great Mother rides the beast.

WHAT IS THE BEAST?

The beast is not a person, but a **teaching authority** promoting all the fertility practices everyone is blind to, though they are in plain sight of everyone. It's Nimrod's wormwood.

The beast is the **reign of Babel**, the teaching authority that will end at the coming of Yahusha's reign. This is why at His coming **the reign** becomes the **reign of Yahusha**. Note Rev. 11:15:

"And the 7th messenger sounded, and there came to be loud voices in the heaven, saying, 'The reign of this world has become *the reign* of our Master, and of His Mashiak, and He shall reign forever and ever!'"

BABEL'S REIGN FALLS

"And he cried with a mighty voice, saying, 'Babel the great is fallen, is fallen, and has become a dwelling place of demons, a haunt for every unclean spirit, and a haunt for every unclean and hated bird, because all the nations have drunk of the wine of the wrath of her whoring, and the sovereigns of the earth have committed whoring with her and the merchants of the earth have become rich through the power of her riotous living.'

And I heard another voice from the heaven saying, 'Come out of her, my people, lest you share in her sins, and lest you receive of her plagues." - Rev 18:2-4

NIMROD'S ASTROLOGICAL WORMWOOD

Birthday celebrations originate from Babel's worship of the host of heaven. They are the foundation of Astrology, and such celebrating is witchcraft. It's the oldest form of idolatry and found in every culture on Earth. All sorcery flows from Babel, and Yahuah shows us how to guard against it in His Torah:

"You do not make for yourself a carved image, or any likeness of that which is in the shamayim above, or which is in the arets beneath, or which is in the mayim under the arets, you do not bow down to them nor serve them. For I, Yahuah your Alahim, am a jealous Al, visiting the crookedness of the fathers on the children to the 3rd and 4th generations of those who hate Me, but showing kindness to thousands, to those who love Me and guard My commands." – Ex. 20

At Yekezqal (Ezekiel) 8:10, **animals** (a zoo, zodiac) are seen on the inner walls of Yahuah's Temple. Before they killed him, Stephen told the Sanhedrin they were **worshipping the host of heaven:**
"So Alahim turned and gave them up to worship the host of the heaven." - Acts 7:42

Nimrod's hunting equipment is a prominent feature:

NIMROD - ORION - SAGITTARIUS
BABEL'S OLD RELIGION
ZODIAC - HOROSCOPE - ASTROLOGY

Nimrod's astrological deities come in a variety of genders and trans-human forms. Consider the Zodiac patterns. The deity of the Philistines was a sea nymph. Dagon brings the star-worship and business plan together in the name STARBUCKS.

ZODIAC MAZZAROTH - The Source Of All Sorcery

The word mazzaroth refers to the host of heaven; a collective term for the sun, moon, planets, quasars, stars, comets, nebulae, and galaxies. The harlot woman, Babel the great, is an idiomatic term for the *teachings* of Babel. It (she) teaches the false worship of the host of heaven, through which all the nations have been deceived. Stephen spoke of it to the Sanhedrin. Rev. 2 refers to it as the **teachings of Izebel.** It is a stronghold that has crept into the hearts of some Natsarim teachers, and is capable of deceiving the elect (chosen ones). Babel's occult (hidden) behavior offends Yahuah. Worshipping (or fearing) the omens of animal shapes thought to be living in the sky, mankind has a long record of idolatry inherited from the astral woman of Revelation 17, Babel.

http://www.fossilizedcustoms.com/zodiac.html

Babel's *teachings* have infected the whole world. Sometimes we hear this woman referred to as "Mother Nature" in the secular media. False behavior and beliefs have been embraced, even by some modern Natsarim.

Some teach that the **secret mystery of deliverance** has been *"written in the stars,"* an idea first published in a 19th-century novel **Mazzaroth** by Francis Rolleston. Alexander Hislop's **Two Babylons** was written to counter some of the false claims made in the book **Mazzaroth**.

The Catholic cardinal John Henry Newman had to respond to Hislop with his own book, **An Essay On The Development of Christian Doctrine.** The theologian Ethelbert William Bullinger believed the false information in **Mazzaroth**, and wrote his own book, **Witness of The Stars.** It shows from Scripture how Yahuah feels about the nations worshipping the host of heaven. Any mixing or **syncretism** (especially the zodiac) arouses His most fierce wrath.

People overlook how Stephen confronted the Sanhedrin with their fascination with the **host of heaven.** We have to stay alert to any false teachings using the constellations to predict the return of Yahusha, or His work of redemption. Syncretism is the mixture of differing beliefs.

The dragon invented the zodiac, but Yahuah made the stars. The message **of deliverance** is not found in the stars, but rather it is found in the prophetic Word of Yahuah. Peter describes the defilements of this deluded kosmic system at 2Pet 2:18-22. We must not return to the corruption as a dog returns to its vomit. The old religion of Babel lures through the enticement of sexual love, and is a scheme of the devil. Compatibility is not directed through horoscopes or magical spells.

There are Christian and Natsarim teachers claiming the "gospel" or message is written in the constellations. Yahusha's **redemption plan** is not recorded in stars, but rather in the Scriptures as shadows through the 7 festivals (appointed times): **Pesach, Matsah, Bikkurim, Shabuoth, Yom Teruah, Yom Kafar, and Sukkoth.**
http://www.fossilizedcustoms.com/redemption.html

Yekezqal (Ezekiel) chapter 8 records that Yahuah's people had forsaken Him by placing these symbols inside His Dwelling Place:
"And I went in and looked and saw all kinds of creeping creatures, abominable beasts, and all the idols of the house of Yisharal, carved all around on the walls." - Ez 8:10
Many synagogues were decorated with **zodiacs** on walls and

floors. The signs of the **Zodiac** are a living **ZOO** of imaginary creatures depicted in the heavens by connecting the dots of stars. Yahuah created the lights to be for signs and seasons. These "signs" are **signals**, not **messages** within themselves. The "signs" signal the appointments which reveal the **redemption plan.** The shadows of things to come are the 7 appointed times (moedim). It is a crafty scheme to shift our attention away from the true shadows of redemption and teach Babel's zodiac signs instead.

Yahuah specifically commanded us to **not** fear the signs of the heavens in the way of the gentiles:
"Thus said Yahuah, 'Do not learn the way of the gentiles, and do not be awed by the signs of the heavens, for the gentiles are awed by them." – Jer/YirmeYahu 10:2

To make Scripture say things it doesn't say is to *feed on wormwood.* Teachers promote the following text as proof that Yahuah used the animal shapes imagined to be in the stars to teach us **the gospel** (as they refer to it): **"The heavens are proclaiming the esteem of Al; and the expanse is declaring the work of His hand. Day to day pours forth speech, and night to night reveals knowledge."** - Ps. 19:1-2

Has Yahuah ever told us to connect the stars into the shapes of animals?

E. W. Bullinger's book, *Witness of the Stars* uses Psalm 19 as a basis, and uses Astrology to confirm Yahuah's Word.

The man was brilliant, but he embraced Babel's zodiac. It was the only knowledge of the skies available to him at the time. Since his time, our understanding has vastly increased.

We've **turned aside to myths**, as Paul warned us at 2Tim 4. Babel's mythological patterns draw us away from true worship. Yahuah tells us: **". . . and lest you lift up your eyes to the heavens, and shall see the sun, and the moon, and the stars all the host of the heavens – and you be drawn away into bowing down to them and serving them, which Yahuah your Alahim has allotted to all the peoples under all the heavens."** – Dt. 4:19

The message of redemption is not found in the shapes and designs imagined to be in the skies, but it's found in the inspired Word of Yahuah.

"And I shall give you shepherds according to My heart, and they shall feed you with knowledge and understanding."
- YirmeYahu 3:15

THE MAGISTERIUM CONTROLS BELIEFS
Babel's controlling authority over what people believe and practice evolved into the totalitarian magisterium the world calls the Roman Catholic Church. It has always been here since the founding of Babel, but has gone by many other names.
The most recent form of this beastly world government grew from its Roman roots, which openly worshipped the Sun deity Apollo Sol Invictus. Constantine merged, or synthesized, diverse Sun worshipping bodies together into a universal pattern of behavior. Mithraism, Zoroastrianism, Hinduism, and Manichaean customs were blended into a new mold, and these pagan forms of witchcraft came together into a new shape. Sun worship has shape-shifted, and can still be found where there are pillars, crosses (solar symbol), and meetings in the morning on the Day of the Sun, Sunday. The book Sunday Origins has more on this:
http://www.fossilizedcustoms.com/sundayorigins.html

This beastly World Order channels Babel's power in three divisions: Clergy-Nobility-Laity. It has been so since the days of Nimrod, the Great Architect of the World Order. This magisterium is Babel going under another name, and all the reigns of the Earth are controlled as surely as a beast is controlled by a ring in its nose. Babel's world government poses as a religious institution. Over the centuries it has set up a list of dogmas and requires its adherents to accept them with absolute devotion. This beast behaves like a chameleon, adopting the practices and symbols of indigenous populations and changing their meaning. Behind all the symbols and practices is the ancient religion of Babel: Sun worship, and the worship of the "host of heaven."
This organization considers itself the only path to salvation through its dogmas. Salvation is understood to be solely through the dispensation of seven sacraments, available exclusively through the priesthood of the "one true mother church." Failure to believe in any one dogma is grounds for excommunication.
For many centuries those who resisted the authority of this mother church were burned at the stake as heretics.

THEY PUBLISH BULLS TO ENFORCE NEW DOCTRINES

This magisterium is the source of such doctrines as **Purgatory, eternal suffering in fire, relic kissing** (veneration of human remains)**, transubstantiation** (bread wafer transforms into living body and blood of Yahusha with words "hoc est corpus meum")**, statue veneration** (kneeling before objects)**, steeples/sun pillars, bells, worship of the "host"** (in a monstrance – sun burst object)**, prayers to the dead** (necromancy via rosaries)**, monks, nuns, popes, priests, celibacy, indulgences, trinity doctrine, infant baptism, apostolic succession, sacraments, crosses** (symbol of Sun deity everywhere throughout history)**, replacement of Name Yahuah to "LORD"** (Baal)**, adoption of Easter / Ishtar fertility festival with sunrise worship & egg/bunny/fish symbols, Natalis Sol Invictus** (Saturnalia) **transformed into "Christ-Mass," a celebration of Yahusha's birth**, - and much more. They are generally doing everything Yahuah ordered not to be done, while ignoring everything He told us to guard and observe. One of the dogmas forbade the commoners (laity) to read or possess the Scriptures.

This magisterium is the source from which Protestants have inherited many of their doctrines and behavior. Universalism (the meaning of the Latin word Catholic) has one defining doctrine.

The belief in *"one god in three persons"* **defines** Catholicism according to Athanasius, one of the attendees of the Nicene Council in 325. Athanasius was from Alexandria's Didascalia (teaching authority), and is dubbed the *"father of orthodoxy."*

Ortho-doxy literally means *"upright teaching."*

The father of wormwood taught him everything he knew.

Natsarim throughout history were considered heretics by the

circus fathers, and were considered to be **anathema**.
Natsarim work to teach the Truth, and reject the teaching authority of the magisterium, and all those following its rebellious practices. Everything listed on the previous page is witchcraft, carefully fed to the masses over many centuries. Abiding in Yahuah's Word sets us free from false beliefs.

The tendency for us to make judgments about what others believe became a **totalitarian magisterium** the world calls the Roman Catholic Church. This beastly World Order is an **authoritarian world government** posing as a religious institution. It has set up a list of dogmas requiring its adherents to accept with absolute devotion. This organization considers itself the only path to salvation through its dogmas.
To not believe in one dogma is grounds for excommunication, and in past centuries this meant death, often by burning at the stake. They were not kidding around about their authority over the whole world.

RISE OF THE JESUIT WORMWOOD
The Protestant Reformation caused the nobility to turn away from the head of this government, wounding it severely to death.
The response to this wounding to the head came immediately through a Spanish soldier named Ignatius de Loyola.
He founded a new society to fight against those opposed to the papacy at Montmartre, France, August 15, 1534.
It was officially recognized by a Papal **Bull** in 1540.
It is a counter-Reformation which Loyola referred to as **Regimini Militantis Ecclesiae**, Latin for *"to the government of the church militant."* The objective of the Societas IESU, or Jesuits, is to restore the authority of the papacy over the world. This would heal the deadly wound inflicted on the fourth beast.

THAT'S A KIND OF BULL I HAVEN'T HEARD IN A VERY LONG TIME

SOUNDS LIKE WORMWOOD TO ME.

THEY LITERALLY JUST MAKE STUFF UP!

A papal bull is a letters-patent named after the lead seal (bulla) it is authenticated by, and is the most solemn documentation of the RCC.

TRANSUBSTANTIATING WORMWOOD BULL

The doctrine of transubstantiation was adopted in the year 1215, and caused many who did not believe it to be burned at the stake by the Inquisitors. It's believed that when an ordained priest utters the Latin words "hoc est corpus meum" (this is my body), a bit of bread and wine miraculously transforms from bread into the living body and blood of Yahusha. They killed all those who did not believe this.
In other words, they are performing a miracle, yet as often as they may do so, such miracles somehow don't count in declaring the priest a "saint."
They believe the substance has changed, but only *appears* to still be bread and wine. How about if they said they'd changed lead into gold, but it still appeared to be lead?
Imagine a bowling ball someone claims changed into a golf ball, yet remained in appearance as a bowling ball. Millions of intelligent adults faithfully believe the doctrine of transubstantiation.
If this *sacrament* is a false teaching, so are all the others.

IS THE WORMWOOD OF THE MAGISTERIUM INFALLIBLE?

The Scriptures are interpreted by the living Spirit of Yahusha in a believer, guiding us into all Truth, not by a hierarchy imposing its authority over us. Yahusha is our only teaching authority, and we are all brothers and sisters. Nicolaitane behavior is hated by Yahusha. The doctrine of "apostolic succession" is a man-made tradition. Because the Natsarim have always ignored the authority of the Roman Circus, we were forced to hide in the valleys (Waldensians). The Alexandrian Cult wrote about us, condemning us for living according to the Torah, seeing no difference between us and the Yahudim, except that we believe in Yahusha. If the Roman Circus is infallible, how did they manage to alter the 4th Commandment, the sign of the eternal Covenant, to the Day of the Sun? Yahuah told us not to erect a pillar anywhere (Lev / Uyiqra 26:1), so the Circus puts them on every building they can find. The infallible aspect seems to pertain to the ability to never miss a chance to disobey. What Yahuah told us to never do, they do. What He told us to do, they avoid like the plague. The reason the reapers are about to be released is because men have broken the everlasting Covenant: **"See, Yahuah is making the Earth empty and making it**

waste, and shall overturn its surface, and shall scatter abroad its inhabitants. And it shall be – as with the people so with the priest, as with the servant so with his master, as with the female servant so with her mistress, as with the buyer so with the seller, as with the lender so with the borrower, as with the creditor so with the debtor; the earth is completely emptied and utterly plundered, for Yahuah has spoken this word.
The Earth shall mourn and wither, the world shall languish and wither, the haughty people of the earth shall languish. For the earth has been defiled under its inhabitants, because they have transgressed the Toroth, changed the law, broken the everlasting Covenant." - YashaYahu 24:15
You can't fix this with holy water, sacraments, and powerless prayers to someone named Jesus, because that's not His Name, and it never will be. His Name is Yahusha, and means *"I am your Deliverer."* Partially translated, it can also mean *"Yah is our Deliverer."* He is Yahuah *incarnate* (literally, *in the flesh*).

There's an incredibly diverse amount of **witchcraft** practiced openly which few people perceive as evil in Yahusha's eyes. Instead of pledging ourselves to invisible genies, wearing wizard caps, baking cakes for the queen of heaven, lighting candles and making wishes, we need to be restored to favor with Yahusha. Paganism is as paganism does. If we practice evil things, we will be barred from the presence of Yahusha, and not be allowed to enter through the gates of the New Yerushalayim.
"Blessed are those doing His commands, so that the authority shall be theirs unto the tree of life, and to enter through the gates into the city. But outside are the dogs and

those who enchant with drugs, and those who whore, and the murderers, and the idolaters, and all who love and do falsehood." – Rev 22:14-15

WHAT IS THE MESSAGE OF YAHUAH?
The **Besorah of Yahuah** is the explanation and solution to the greatest question, mankind's oldest mystery: Why are we here? The explanation tells us the purpose of life: ***to learn to love***. **Active love** is **serving**. From beginning to end, the Creator has pleaded, searched hearts, and repeated Himself beyond measure for mankind to return to Him. Who has ears to hear Him? He said, **"Love Me, and guard My Commandments."** The Word, Light, Wisdom, Living Water, and His Covenant are all the same thing: the **Turah of Yahuah**. Turah teaches **how** to love, but most people try to bear the fruit without the instructions. Torah is Truth, Yahuah's Word. We can't skip it or sneak in some other way. It is the Gate, and the Gate is Yahusha Himself. We accept Him as our Redeemer and Sovereign, and show Him by obeying His Commandments. There is no other way to worship Him; He only accepts obedience, our reasonable worship.

CREATION'S PURPOSE: LOVE
The Mashiak of Israel, Yahusha of Natsarith, told an elder:
"If you do not believe when I spoke to you about earthly things, how are you going to believe when I speak to you about the heavenly things? And no one has gone up into the heavens except He who came down from the heavens – the Son of Adam. And as Mosheh lifted up the serpent in the wilderness, even so must the Son of Adam be lifted up, so that whosoever believes in Him should not perish but possess everlasting life. For Alahim so loved the world that He gave His only procreated Son, so that everyone who believes in Him should not perish but possess everlasting life. For Alahim did not send His Son into the world to judge the world, but that the world through Him might be saved. He who believes in Him is not judged, but he who does not believe is judged already, because he has not believed in the Name of the only procreated Son of Alahim. And this is the judgment, that the light has come into the world, and men loved the darkness rather than the light, for their works were evil. For everyone who practices evil hates

the light and does not come to the light, lest his works should be exposed. But the one doing the truth comes to the light, so that his works are clearly seen, that they have been wrought in Alahim." – Yn. 3

Yahusha does not want any to perish.

"For Alahim so loved the world that He gave His only brought-forth Son, so that everyone who believes in Him should not perish but possess everlasting life.

For Alahim did not send His Son into the world to judge the world, but that the world through Him might be saved. He who believes in Him is not judged, but he who does not believe is judged already, because he has not believed in the Name of the only brought-forth Son of Alahim.

And this is the judgment, that the Light has come into the world, and men loved the darkness rather than the Light, for their works were wicked. For everyone who is practicing evil matters hates the Light and does not come to the Light, lest his works should be exposed. But the one doing the truth comes to the Light, so that his works are clearly seen, that they have been wrought in Alahim." - Yn. 3:16-2

WORMWOOD IS TRADITION

"And He answering, said to them, 'Well did YashaYahu prophesy concerning you hypocrites, as it has been written, "This people respect Me with their lips, but their heart is far from Me. And in vain do they worship Me, teaching as teachings the commands of men." Forsaking the Command of Alahim, you hold fast the tradition of men.' And He said to them, 'Well do you set aside the command of Alahim, in order to guard your tradition.'" - Mark 7:6-9

With Yahusha's words in ringing in your mind, what traditions may have come to replace the Commands of Yahuah?

Try these on for size:

Christmas; Easter; Sunday; Halloween (feast of dead saints); sacraments; steeples; bells; crosses; eating unclean animals; apostolic succession; celibacy; veneration of human remains, images; holy water; indulgences; trinitarian ideas; prayer beads; prohibition of true Name, Yahuah, Yahusha; prayers to the dead (necromancy); infant baptism; and much more. Men have set aside the Commands of Yahuah for their traditions, turning His Word into wormwood. Time is almost up.

THE DAY OF YAHUAH WILL BE JUDGMENT DAY
This is the day Babel's reign ends, and Yahusha's reign begins.

JUDGMENT DAY **EAGLES ARE COMING** DO YOU KNOW WHO THEY ARE?

"For wherever the dead body is, there the eagles shall be gathered together . . . And immediately after the distress of those days, the sun shall be darkened, and the moon shall not give its light, and the stars shall fall from the heaven, and the powers of the heavens shall be shaken." – Mt. 24:28-29 **"Whoever calls upon the Name of Yahuah will be delivered."** Statements found at Yual (Joel) 2 & Acts 2
The reason they will be delivered is: They are sealed with the Name of Yahusha. Our Owner places **His Name** on His property so the REAPERS will not harm what belongs to Him.

Our Redeemer is coming and the fallen malakim know their time is short. People believing in a pre-Trib rapture will make some adjustments in their expectations, and come to accept the reality unfolding around them. Most of them today are Sun-day Sabbath people, and many are becoming **Natsarim** (Acts 24:5), end-time harvest workers. Our most important work during the time of distress will be to help them be restored to the Covenant of Yahuah, the message of AliYahu. (Mal 4:1-6)
"But the Day of Yahuah shall come as a thief in the night, in which the heavens shall pass away with a great noise, and the elements shall melt with intense heat, and the earth and the works that are in it shall be burned up." - 2Pe 3:10
"And the present heavens and the Earth are treasured up by the same Word, being kept for fire, to a day of judgment and destruction of wicked men." - 2Pe 3:7
"And now, be wise, O sovereigns; be instructed, you rulers of the Earth. Serve Yahuah with fear, and rejoice with trembling. Kiss the Son, lest He be enraged, and you perish in the way, for soon His wrath is to be kindled. Blessed are all those taking refuge in Him." - Ps 2:10-12 - See Acts 17:30-31

THE FINAL WARNING TO ALL MANKIND

"Remember the Torah of Mosheh, My servant, which I commanded him in Horeb for all Yisharal – laws and right-rulings. See, I am sending you AliYahu the prophet before the coming of the great and awesome day of Yahuah. And he shall turn the hearts of the fathers to the children, and the hearts of the children to their fathers, lest I come and smite the arets with utter destruction." - Mal 4:4-6

After the reapers come, we'll be snatched-away just as the Scriptures describe, but it will be at the end of the Distress. Mt 24:29-31

Yahusha explained how He would send His malakim to the ends of the Earth to gather His elect, so we won't be using transports of any human design. As part of **our** preparation to endure the Distress, Yahusha foretold certain events. He specifically described the darkening of the Sun. Most people reject our words now, but a time is coming when they will beg to listen. *Events will occur that no one will be able to ignore.* Everyone not sealed for protection - *Elitists, homosexuals, secular humanists, abortionists, atheists, agnostics, the media, and those who practice false religion* - will experience a breakdown in their sanity. Reading *Harry Potter* books won't help anyone with what's coming. Minds will snap, and hearts will melt within all mankind.

Because we know His Name, Yahusha wants us, His body, to be aware of coming events in order to spare us the terrible **fear** that others will face. Read Ps 91 as it relates to what you are about to learn.

Kepha/Peter quoted the prophet Yual/Joel in Acts 2 describing the end of days: *"And I shall give signs in the heavens and upon the Earth: blood and fire and columns of smoke; the sun is turned into darkness, and the moon into blood, before the coming of the great and awesome Day of Yahuah. And it shall be that everyone who calls on the Name of Yahuah shall be delivered. For on Mount Tsiyon and in Yerushalayim there shall be an escape as Yahuah has said, and among the survivors whom Yahuah calls."*
- Yual 2:30-32; also Act 2:21,2:39; Rom 10:13, Isa 4:2-3, Obad v. 17, Rev. 14:1.

The most frightening thing for everyone alive on this planet will be the sudden darkening of the Sun.

We are told in advance about this severe sign *so that we would not be afraid*. Many people will simply drop dead when they experience the fright of the Sun turning dark.

THE REALITY ALL AROUND US

The sun is in *equilibrium*, balanced between the outward pressure of its thermonuclear process and the inward gravitational pull caused by its mass. The phrase *"moon into blood"* describes an optical principal of the light spectrum. When the sun goes out, it will be Yahuah temporarily stopping the thermonuclear activity deep inside the sun, where hydrogen is constantly being converted into helium (fusion), under extreme pressure and temperature.

It's like a constant outward explosion from the core of the sun. When this process stops, the *photosphere* (visible shell of glowing gas) of the Sun will undergo an immediate spectral change toward the red, and the gas ball will utterly go out like a campfire. It will still glow very brightly in the red part of the spectrum from the sheer **heat** stored in its core and outer regions. This is what will make the moon seem to be the color of **blood**, reflecting the light from the reddened sun.

The heliosphere, or solar wind, will essentially cease to exist.

The Sun will have become a red-dwarf star.

Because the outward pressure will temporarily stop, the Sun's mass will cause it to shrink to less than half its current perceived size. As scary as this whole scenario sounds, what follows is even worse. When the sun re-ignites from the pressure of the collapsing gas, there will be a solar nova, or burst of heat, light, and plasma. This will seriously scorch the Earth, and many will be burned to a crisp. The oceans will be moved out of their places, and islands will be annihilated. Coastlands will be lashed clean. All of these things have been described by the prophets of Yahuah, and Yahusha also warned us of them (Mt 24). Kefa (Peter) spoke of it also, at 2 Pet. chapters 2 & 3.

This outpouring of **wrath** on the rebellious will not harm those steadfast in the Covenant, for we will be changed, clothed with immortality, just as these events begin to unfold.

"A thousand fall at your side, and ten thousand at your right hand; but it does not come near you." - Ps 91:7

We are guarded by messengers now. It will become obvious in

the distress:

"No evil befalls you, and a plague does not come near your tent; for He commands His messengers concerning you, to guard you in all your ways." Ps 91:10,11 (tent = your body). We will be protected from even stubbing our toe on the **Day of Yahuah.**

Extending over the entire Earth, it will be like the *plague of darkness* in the land of Egypt. Added to all this excitement, "stars" (meteors) will fall from the sky, causing some to blaspheme Yahuah. Some of these meteors will be near planet-killers, causing the Earth to reel like a drunkard from the breaking up of the crust, exposing magma. It will literally be the worst period seen since the Earth was created. Those living anywhere within hundreds of miles of a volcano or crustal plate edge will be **consumed by lava**. Yahusha promised to shorten the days for our sakes. Then He will appear in the skies, and every eye will see Him coming. The transgressors and those who resist His Sovereignty will be hiding themselves in the caves, and under rocks, in tunnels they've prepared.

"And the fourth messenger poured out his bowl on the Sun, and it was given to him to burn men with fire. And men were burned with great heat, and they blasphemed the Name of Alahim Who possesses authority over these plagues. And they did not repent, to give Him esteem." - Rev 16:8,9

The Sun will burn mankind.

"Howl, for the day of Yahuah is near! It comes as a destruction from the Almighty. Therefore all hands go limp, every man's heart melts, and they shall be afraid. Pangs and sorrows take hold of them, they are in pain as a woman in labor; They are amazed at one another, their faces aflame! See, the day of Yahuah is coming, fierce, with wrath and heat of displeasure, to lay the Earth waste, and destroy its sinners from it." - YashaYahu / Isa 13:6-9

False teachings about *when* we will be changed cause many people to believe they will not be on Earth to witness the wrath. Rather, we will be taken (or snatched) by Yahusha as He is returning in the skies, coming to take dominion over this lost world. Our Redeemer comes to take us to Himself, so we must not fear the wrath being poured out. As the lost will feel the terror, we will feel the love of His presence as He comes to gather us on the day of His return.

Look carefully at each component of the following text, describing the Distress, followed by the **gathering** of the qodeshim. Mat 24:29-31:

"And immediately after the distress of those days the sun shall be darkened, and the moon shall not give its light, and the stars shall fall from the heaven, and the powers of the heavens shall be shaken.

And then the sign of the Son of Adam shall appear in the heaven, and then all the tribes of the Earth shall mourn, and they shall see the Son of Adam coming on the clouds of the heaven with power and much esteem.

And He shall send His messengers with a great sound of a trumpet, and they shall gather together His chosen ones from the four winds, from one end of the heavens to the other."

If you noticed, these events describe a period of distress (Great Trib), followed by the grand finale, the darkening of the sun. Next, a meteorite bombardment commences, and the powers of the heavens "shake". *"And then"*, Yahusha appears in the skies, apparently while the sun remains darkened. At this point, a great "shofar" is heard, and the messengers (malakim) are sent to gather the chosen ones (elect). It is at this point the sealed Torah-obedient followers of Yahusha are really gathered. It should be obvious to all readers now; the Christian "rapture" ideas are incorrect, and are dangerous because so many will be unproductive harvest workers, paralyzed by the false expectations they were given. Yahusha wants them to return to the Covenant NOW, so they might be added to us to do His work among the lost in the days ahead.

" . . . pray the Master of the harvest to send out workers into His harvest." - Lk 10:2

The majority of Christians have been listening to poisonous teachings, making them unprepared to stand in the day of wrath. These are the survivors whom Yahuah will call, *assisted by the Natsarim who will be on Earth during the distress.* The Natsarim are the elect (chosen ones) for whom the **duration** of the distress will be shortened.

Our purpose during the distress will be to help people be restored to the Covenant. They must be helped to overcome many false teachings learned from misguided preachers. They will learn that Sun-day is *not the day Yahuah blessed*, and because of their distress, *they will listen to us more closely*. They will not argue about the true Name, and many will submit to immersion for the remission of sin, and be sealed for protection.

THE DAY OF YAHUAH IS COMING

"For this we say to you by the Word of the Master, that we, the living who are left over at the coming of the Master shall in no way go before those who are asleep. Because the Master Himself shall come down from heaven with a shout, with the voice of a chief messenger, and with the trumpet of Alahim, and the dead in Mashiak shall rise first. Then we, the living who are left over, shall be caught away together with them in the clouds to meet the Master in the air – and so we shall always be with the Master. So, then, encourage one another with these words." - 1Th 4:15, 16

"'For look, the day shall come, burning like a furnace, and all the proud, and every wrongdoer shall be stubble. And the day that shall come shall burn them up,' said Yahuah Tsabaoth, 'which leaves to them neither root nor branch. But to you who fear My Name, the Servant of Righteousness shall arise with healing in His wings. And you shall go out and leap for joy like calves from the stall. And you shall trample the wrongdoers, for they shall be ashes under the soles of your feet on the day that I do this,' said Yahuah Tsabaoth. Remember the Torah of Mosheh, My servant, which I commanded him in Horeb for all Yisharal – laws and right-rulings. See, I am sending you AliYahu the prophet before the coming of the great and awesome Day of Yahuah. And he shall turn the hearts of the fathers to the children, and the hearts of the children to their fathers, lest I come and smite the Earth with utter destruction.'" - Mal 4:1-6

The world is loaded with wormwood, the leaven of men. **The leaven represents the traditions of men. Our freedom is from the traditions of men**, which Yahusha was the most critical of above all else. Yahusha calls the teachings of men **leaven**. He was never upset because anyone obeyed the Ten Commandments, but rather because they disobeyed them and made men's traditions their commandments.

The seven-day observance called Unleavened Bread (Matsah) is a shadow of redemption that pictures the removal of the **moldy, puffed-up teaching authority of men from our hearts**, so **our hearts** are able to receive the pure, clean teachings of Yahusha, free of the corrupting ideas of men. Yahusha was upset with how traditions came to replace the Commandments of Yahuah.

If Yahusha were to appear in person at a Sunday morning assembly, He would surely see nothing that reflects how He taught us to live, because Constantine insisted that they would have **"nothing in common with the hostile rabble of the Yahudim."** Most still have **Constantine's** mold in their hearts. This is a small glimpse at the **festival of Matsah**, one of seven observances of Yahuah.

For more information on the festivals, see www.torahzone.net

WHO IS OUR IDEAL ROLE MODEL?

The only role model we can have is Yahusha, all others will disappoint us. We shouldn't wait to be a role model, we must focus on being a servant. All of the people Yahuah uses are imperfect vessels, but in our weakness, His power is perfected. Abraham lied about Sarai when he claimed she was "only" his sister, implying she was not his wife. Actually, both were true, but he deceived the Mitsrites by withholding that she was also his wife, in order that they would not kill him to have her.

Yahusha is developing our personality into His own.

When He fully inhabits us at His coming, our personality will be completely His. Keep working. We're soldiers in a battle.

We're not putting up asherim, we're taking them down!

We dismantle all strongholds and false reasonings.

O, WHAT A TANGLED WEB WE WEAVE WHEN FIRST WE PRACTICE TO DECEIVE
- Walter Scott   TORAHZONE.NET

YOU'RE IN THE MOTHER OF HARLOTS BABELZONE
STARBUCKS COFFEE
FERTILITY IN YOUR FACE
DAGON OF THE PHILISTINES
TORAH INSTITUTE

Nimrod's Star-Religion is all about fertility.
The sea nymph DAGON is another babbled name for Nimrod.
If you haven't detected the leaven, look for the stars and fish.
Notice how fertility is being expressed in the logo above.

YAHUAH EXPLAINS IT TO US
"And it shall be, when you declare to this people all these
words, and they shall say to you, 'Why has Yahuah
pronounced all this great evil against us? And what is our
crookedness, and what is our sin that we have committed
against Yahuah our Alahim?' then you shall say to them,
'Because your fathers have forsaken Me,' declares Yahuah,
'and have walked after other mighty ones and served them
and bowed themselves to them, and have forsaken Me, and
did not guard My Turah. And you have done more evil than
your fathers, for look, each one walks according to the
stubbornness of his own evil heart, without listening to Me.
So I shall throw you out of this land into a land that you do
not know, neither you nor your fathers. And there you shall
serve other mighty ones yom and lailah, where I show you
no favor.' Therefore see, the Yomim are coming," declares
Yahuah, "when it is no longer said, 'Yahuah lives who
brought up the children of Yisharal from the land of
Mitsrayim,' but, 'Yahuah lives who brought up the children
of Yisharal from the land of the north and from all the lands
where He had driven them.' For I shall bring them back into
their land I gave to their fathers. See, I am sending for many
fishermen," declares Yahuah, "and they shall fish them. And
after that I shall send for many hunters, and they shall hunt
them from every mountain and every hill, and out of the
holes of the rocks. For My eyes are on all their ways; they
have not been hidden from My face, nor has their
crookedness been hidden from My eyes.
And first I shall repay double for their crookedness and their
sin, because they have defiled My land with the dead bodies
of their disgusting things, and have filled My inheritance
with their abominations." O Yahuah, my strength and my
stronghold and my refuge, in the yom of distress the
gentiles shall come to You from the ends of the arets and
say, "Our fathers have inherited only falsehood, futility, and

there is no value in them."
Would a man make mighty ones for himself, which are not mighty ones? Therefore see, I am causing them to know, this time I cause them to know My hand and My might. And they shall know that My Name is Yahuah!'" - YirmeYahu 16:10-21

THE HUNTERS ARE SHOWING UP NOW

ALL WHO HATE ME LOVE DEATH

"And now, listen to me, you children, for blessed are they who guard my ways. Listen to discipline and become wise, and do not refuse it. Blessed is the man who listens to me, watching daily at my gates*, waiting at the posts of my doors.* For whoever finds me shall find life, and obtain favor from Yahuah. But he who sins against me injures himself. All who hate me love death!" - Proverbs 8:32-36
*The Ten Commandments are written on the doorposts and gates.

If you stop to think carefully about it, you will recall how there were several people Yahusha used to pursue you.

What condition would you be in if you had not had someone sent to tell you that you were dead in sin, and convicted you of it? Eventually you turned from sinning, and began to feel alive for the first time. Yahusha had come into you, and you continued to grow stronger each day. The more you allow Him to clean your vessel, the more purified your heart becomes and you become like Him.

We see the world as filled with zombies, and we remember that we were once one of them. **We are awakened among them**, and being awakened now, we feel very alone.

When we encounter another follower of Yahusha, we prefer to be with them rather than go back out into the world among the zombies. But they will perish if we don't let Yahusha hunt them. Yahusha came into a world of zombies to seek and to save. We are His ambassadors, envoys bringing light into the darkness. Wormwood is still active, even among some teachers. There are movements arising now among the Natsarim trying to compel like-minded believers to **move together** so they will be close to others who they can fellowship with all the time.

The last days are here, and our time must be spent primarily seeking the people in need of life, rather than spending the little time we have left fine-tuning how we perceive those who are teaching us. We are hearing more talk from teachers that want their congregations to grow in attendance, and they are asking people to move closer to their locations so everyone can live in communities with believers where there are few zombies.

Who, then, will go to be among the zombies? The zombies need us to be speaking to them, and we are already living among them.

DISTORTED TEACHINGS TO DRAW YOU AWAY

"Also from among yourselves men shall arise, speaking distorted *teachings* to draw away talmidim after themselves." – Acts 20:30

Teaching apocalypticism in the sense that Yahusha's return is imminent is Scripturally correct. The tendency to run away from the lost people of the world is not. If we are cowardly as the **Day of Yahuah** approaches, and more concerned for ourselves than the lost, we serve our own purpose, not Yahusha's.

Many are being lured into thinking they can best serve Yahusha if they run away from their mission and be set-apart from the world.

This thinking is behind other faith communities of the past: Jim Jones' *Peoples Temple*, David Koresh's *Branch Davidians*, and *Heavens Gate* are among several notorious examples of large groups who were told to move together by their leader, and wasted their lives for no reason. Ravenous wolves taught them false teachings as Paul warned us they would at Acts 20:30. Men teach nothing Yahuah commanded us to live by. He said not to eat pigs (Lev. 11) or erect pillars (Lev. 26), so that's exactly what men do. They've eaten wormwood for too long.

WHAT DID YAHUSHA TELL US TO DO?

How should we feel about the idea that all of us move close to one another so we can be together and away from the lawless unbelievers? Is this what Yahusha did, and what He told us to do? Some want to move to the land in advance of the regathering at the coming of Yahusha. Others are induced to move to other places just to be around other Torah-observant believers. There is a time coming when we will all live with other Torah people: when Yahusha returns to those who belong to Him.

For now, we are salted among the lost. If we leave from where Yahusha awakened us, those who are lost around us will perish and we will have abandoned our post. Don't be lured away from where you were planted, stay at your post.

If we are drawn away from where Yahusha planted us in order to be around one another, we would be bunched-up together and going on with our own happy goals, and be of no use to the lost.

We are not sent to the well, we are sent to the sick.

For 37 years I labored among New Agers, Hindus, witches, murderers, thieves, drug addicts, and lost Christians. Yahusha used that to draw many from their way to follow Torah to become fellow laborers in the harvest.

Many times I've been invited to move to a community of other Torah-observant folks, sometimes out of my native country. If I had done so, those Yahusha intended for me to find would have been abandoned. Don't put the Light under a basket.

Be Yahusha's Light right where you are by allowing Yahusha to use you to sow His seeds of love, the Ten Commandments.

He is the Sower, and He uses us to plant because we are His laborers in His wheat field.

Remain a faithful servant, and wait for the day He will allow us to all be together in one place - the *Marriage Supper of the Lamb* - to *celebrate our marriage* to the Sovereign of the Universe.

Sow the Word, teaching the Word and the Name to all nations.

"This is written for a generation to come, so that a people to be created praise Yah. For He looked down from the height of His set-apart place; from heaven Yahuah viewed the arets, to hear the groaning of the prisoner, to release those appointed to death, to declare the Name of Yahuah in Tsiyon

and His praise in Yerushalayim, when peoples gather together, and reigns, to serve Yahuah." - Psalm 102:18-22

YAHUSHA IS THE ZOMBIE HUNTER WORKING IN HIS NATSARIM
HE SOWS & WATERS THROUGH US.
WE MUST BE PATIENT AND TRUST HE WILL COMPLETE HIS WORK IN THEM.
DON'T EXPECT THE FRUIT TO APPEAR TOO SOON.

HOW THE WORLD LEARNED ENGLISH

The colonies of the British Empire brought the English language to the whole world, and today it's the language of all business. The KJV helped kick-start the process of teaching English all around the world, yet the famine (Amus 8:11) of His Word remained because the Name was removed and the Covenant resisted by the teachers of the Word. The famine is lifting and many are now hearing His calling **"through a jabbering lip and a foreign tongue."** - Isaiah / YashaYahu 28:11

In English, the Besorah (message) is going forth into the world:
"For 'everyone who calls on the Name of Yahuah shall be saved.' How then shall they call on Him in whom they have not believed? And how shall they believe in Him of whom they have not heard? And how shall they hear without one proclaiming? And how shall they proclaim if they are not sent? As it has been written, 'How pleasant are the feet of those who bring the Besorah of peace, who bring the Besorah of the good!'" - Romans 10:13-15

BEWARE THE BLOB

BEWARE THE LEAVEN OF THE PHARISEES

The 1958 movie, The Blob, could be a metaphor for how religion takes on a life of its own, and everyone is absorbed into it.
The purpose of its existence is to make more of itself.
YirmeYahu 16:19 shows we've inherited lies through traditions. Religion is tradition, and it develops over time as it corrupts itself by men guided by their minds of flesh.
He created each of us to be His companions, and His Torah is instruction for us how to love Him, and how to love our neighbor.

Torah points to the ideal relationship for bearing the perfect fruit of good behavior.
Ecumenical means "world-wide" and promotes the blending together of all faiths under one unified entity. The New World Order seeks the same thing politically and economically.
The centralization of authoritarian control is not hidden, but is in plain sight: the **UN**.
An "initiative" of the UN is called the U.R.I. - United Religions Initiative.
The Catholic pope (Francis, Jorge Mario Bergoglio) is working diligently to strengthen the ecumenical unification of all faith groups, more than anyone before him. Most of us know all about "being in the blob."
We were in the blob until Yahusha called us out of it. Now our minds are controlled by Him, not the blob.

99

This new article may help many people awaken to what they are trapped in. Strongholds of thought hold people's minds captive until they can reach outside their prison and take hold of the Truth. Being in the blob is a metaphor for being controlled by the beast. The beast compels everyone to obey it, and is in opposition to the Covenant of Yahuah. Yahusha is releasing the captives, and restoring us to His Covenant of love.

Religious tradition is the Blob, blindly performing its purpose of absorbing, growing, and competing for dominance.

The **Covenant** is the **marriage** we will celebrate at the **marriage supper**, and *the Blob serves the purpose of annihilating it.*

Our choice: the **Covenant** (life), or the **Blob** (death).

The **BLOB** is the **beast**, or **World Order** begun by Nimrod.

RABBINICAL JUDAISM

Question: What is the leaven, or yeast of the Pharisees?

Answer: Rabbinic Judaism, the traditions of the fathers.

WHERE DID THE IDEA OF A RABBI COME FROM?

A guide to reach fulfillment, or **guru**, came from the culture of Hinduism. This reached the Middle East about the 2nd century BCE. It came from India by way of the trade route known as the *Silk Road*.

"Yoking with forces" to achieve higher chakra levels, and "four levels of interpretation" both originate from Hinduism. Mosheh, Danial, and all other prophets never mentioned the rabbi.

NICOLAITANES AND SELF-EXALTED MEN

Are teachers trying to convince you of codes, numerical secrets, higher levels of knowledge, or that you need the covering of another "enlightened" man?

At Yahusha's return, all rabbis but One will become extinct.

If rabbis are never recommended in Scripture, nor will they be around after Yahusha returns, why are people pretending they need rabbis?

Yahusha is our covering, and His blood redeems us completely. Paul referred to his *"former way of living"* in Yahudaism (the traditions of the fathers, Galatians 1:13), which was the way of the rabbi, called **rabbinical Judaism** today. The prophet YirmeYahu (Jeremiah) informs us how the gentiles will awaken to the Truth in the last days:

"O Yahuah, my strength and my stronghold and my refuge, in the day of distress the gentiles shall come to You from the ends of the earth and say,
'Our fathers have inherited only falsehood, futility, and there is no value in them.'" – YirmeYahu 16:19
(Ps. 147:19, Isa. 2:3, Isa. 60:2-3, John 4:22, Rom. 2:20, Rom. 3:2, Rom. 9:4)

Rules made by men have superseded the Commandments of Yahuah. We are not to add rules or do what seems right in our own eyes:
Dt. 4:2: **"Do not add to the Word which I command you, and do not take away from it, so as to guard the commands of Yahuah your Alahim which I am commanding you."**
(See also Dt. 12:32, Prov. 30:6, Rev. 22:18-19)
Yahusha spoke of how men's traditions replaced Yahuah's Word:
"And He answering, said to them, 'Well did YashaYahu prophesy concerning you hypocrites, as it has been written, "This people respect Me with their lips, but their heart is far from Me. And in vain do they worship Me, teaching as teachings the commands of men."' - Mark 7:6-7
The sandy foundation of men's opinions will not stand:
"For I bear witness that they have an ardour for Alahim, but not according to knowledge. For not knowing the righteousness of Alahim, and seeking to establish their own righteousness, they did not subject themselves to the righteousness of Alahim." - Romans 10:2-3
Rather than wearing the tsitsith (Dt. 22, Num. 15), men invent "standards" like wearing long-sleeve white shirts with a tie before they are allowed to teach in their assemblies. They call Yahuah's Word "the Bible," eat swine's flesh, and profane His Shabath.
We must not be of different opinions, or divided. - 1Kor 1:10
The world is overtaken by religious traditions.
Yunah in Nineveh did not warn them to obey **traditions**, and neither did AliYahu (aka Elijah) *or Yahusha*.
The message must never change: *Repent, or perish!*
Our responsibility remains to warn others when they are out-of-bounds. **"See to it that no one makes a prey of you through philosophy and empty deceit, according to the tradition of men, according to the elementary matters of the world, and not according to Mashiak."** - Kol 2:8

YAHUSHA'S YOKE (teachings, witness, testimony)
1. Love Yahuah with your whole heart, mind, and being.
2. Love your neighbor as yourself.
Yahusha's Word will never pass away, but men's words are like chaff the wind blows away.
Many things will not survive the Second Coming.
The 7-day week will still exist, but we will not be calling the days by the names of pagan deities. We have to decide between tradition (religion) and Truth (reality).
Get rid of the leaven of men's teachings now, they won't survive the Second Coming.

MARK OF THE BEAST: BUYING AND SELLING
From sundown to sundown, our household does no buying and selling, cooking, or traveling unless there's an emergency that threatens life or property. Yahusha spoke of the **last days** (Mt. 24) telling His followers to pray their flight not be in winter or on a Shabath. The **Day of Yahuah** will come on the most solemn annual day of rest, **Yom Kafar**, in the 7th moon one year.
It's called "the FAST" at Acts ~~28:11~~ → *27:9* ☺
Reapers (eagles, the seraphim) will remove the weeds first, then gather the wheat into the barn (New Yerushalayim).
Reapers; more about them:
http://www.fossilizedcustoms.com/reapers.html
Rev. 13 is a riddle, and the **mark** concerns **buying and selling**. Those not having wisdom (Torah) cannot calculate the meaning of the riddle. The reign of Babel (the beast) has Nimrod's mark, as he was worshipped as the Sun. **Sunday** is his mark of authority over the world system, the beast.
http://www.fossilizedcustoms.com/mark.html
www.fossilizedcustoms.com/3estates.html
"Let no man therefore judge you in meat, or in drink, or in respect of a festival, or of the new moon, or of the Shabath days which are a <u>shadow</u> of things to come for the body of Mashiak." - Kol 2:16-17 — See also Is 8:20

Heaven and Earth are still here (see Mt. 5:18), so every letter of the Torah endures to this day. Pastors use Hebrews 7 to tell us the "law was changed." Hebrews 7 tells us the change of law of sacrifices (as covering sins) has come about through our new Kohen ha Gadol, Yahusha, of another tribe (Yahudah).

The Torah (instructions) - the Covenant of lovingkindness - is an eternal one, unchanging, and perfect. Ps. 119 tells us this many times, and verse 165 states:

"Great peace have those loving Your Torah, And for them there is no stumbling-block."

The guarding of the Ten Commandments (obedience) is better than sacrifice (of the old law of sacrifices), and this obedience is never called "filthy rags." The point made at YashaYahu (Is.) 64:6 is that what men call "righteousness" is uncleanness to Yahuah. We've invented our own righteousness, and departed from the old paths in which to walk.

Yahusha is coming to burn the Earth for one reason:

"For the Earth has been defiled under its inhabitants, because they have transgressed the Toroth, changed the law, broken the everlasting Covenant." - YashaYahu / Isa 24:5

www.fossilizedcustoms.com/toxictorah.html

Jer. / YirmeYahu 10:1-5: **"Hear what Yahuah says to you, O house of Yisharal. This is what Yahuah says: 'Do not learn the ways of the nations or be terrified by signs in the sky, though the nations are terrified by them. For the customs of the peoples are worthless; they cut a tree out of the forest, and a craftsman shapes it with his chisel. They adorn it with silver and gold; they fasten it with hammer and nails so it will not totter. Like a scarecrow in a melon patch, their idols cannot speak; they must be carried because they cannot walk. Do not fear them; they can do no harm, nor can they do any good."**

Deut 12:29-32:

"Yahuah your Alahim will cut off before you the nations you are about to invade and dispossess. But when you have driven them out and settled in their land, and after they have been destroyed before you, be careful not to be ensnared by inquiring about their Alahim, saying, "How do these nations serve their Alahim? We will do the same." You must not worship Yahuah your Alahim in their way, because in worshiping their Alahim, they do all kinds of detestable things Yahuah hates. They even burn their sons and daughters in the fire as sacrifices to their Alahim." (i.e., Molok)

THIS BOOK SAYS WE ARE NEVER TO SPEAK THE NAME

THIS BOOK SAYS WE ARE TO PROCLAIM THE NAME

MAN'S WORD

YAHUAH'S WORD

Deut 16:21-22:

"Do not set up any wooden Asherah pole beside the altar you build to Yahuah your Alahim, and do not erect a sacred stone, for these Yahuah your Alahim hates."

Learn NOT the ways of the heathen, and do not bring a detestable thing into your home!

Deut 7:26:

"Do not bring a detestable thing into your house or you, like it, will be set apart for destruction. Utterly abhor and detest it, for it is set apart for destruction."

We are soldiers mightily equipped for tearing-down strongholds.

SCHEME OF THE DEVIL: TO HIDE WITCHCRAFT IN PLAIN SIGHT

TEACHINGS OF PROPHETESS ISEBEL – REV. 2

SUN PILLAR

SHAMMASH

ASHERAH CIRCE

TAMMUZ ASHERAH CIRCE

OBELISK, CONE OF POWER, IMAGE OF JEALOUSY

"And He said to me, 'Son of man, do you see what they are doing, the great abominations which the house of Yisharal are doing here, driving Me away from My set-apart place? And you are to see still greater abominations." Ez. 8:6

WITCHCRAFT IS CALLED CHURCH - KIRKE

The secret of lawlessness in one word: WORMWOOD
They will tell you, "It doesn't mean that to me."
Please don't eat the wormwood.

"Do not make idols for yourselves and do not set up
a carved image or a pillar for yourselves, and do not place
a stone image in your land, to bow down to it. For I am Yahuah your Alahim."

ONLY YAHUSHA CAN RESTORE EYESIGHT TO THE BLIND
RECEIVE YAHUSHA'S TORAHVISION
HE IS OUR ONLY TEACHING AUTHORITY

Do not eat pigs; Lev. 11
Do not erect pillars anywhere in your land; see Lev. 26:1

YAHUSHA WILL END IT

THE MOST DANGEROUS PLACE ON EARTH

Being "mortal" means we are vulnerable to injury and death.
In my research for the video RACIAL STRONGHOLD, a very
disturbing statistic emerged. For all the catagories of recorded
deaths, by far the greatest reason was abortion.
The most dangerous place to be is in your mother's womb.
Yahuah made a specific ordinance concerned with protecting the
unborn at Exodus 21:22-25.
It is three times worse if the mother is black. Margaret Sanger
established a eugenics program with the help of the
Rockefellers, and it is now an international organization known
as Planned Parenthood. One of its chief objectives is to wipe out
the black race. You can research this fact by seeing Sanger's
quotes on the Internet. Genocide is going on right in our midst,
and they place their clinics in the areas where the black
population is most dense. There are many other societal
problems discussed in this important video on youtube.

Watch Racial Identity here:
http://www.youtube.com/watch?v=Wuo2rE8Px4w

THE EASTER HARLOT'S BABYLONIAN ROOTS

Ishtar / Easter promotes Nimrod's rebellion against Yahuah.
Her effigies portray Sun worship, with overtones of freedom and
liberty. She is the Harlot of Babel, and a symbol of lawlessness.
Christian teachers are scrambling to recover from what could be
the greatest "wardrobe malfunction" for the Mother of Harlots.
It's the connection between the name **Ishtar** and **Easter**.

About 1985, I began to study Scripture as a theological archaeologist. Just below the surface of every familiar term and custom there was a filthy core hiding behind a candy-coating. These discoveries inspired the book, Fossilized Customs.

The author Alexander Hislop (Two Babylons) was also a theological archaeologist whose eyes were opened to the connection between Nimrod's reign and the 4th beast, Rome's Magisterium. He drew the connection between the words Easter and Ishtar, yet his critics claim that **phonetics** (the sound of words) is a worthless proof. A rose by any other name is still a rose.

When proper names are concerned, is that really the case, or is the proof too overwhelming to face for those who risk losing their position in a false teaching authority? The Anglican Catholic KJV is the only English translation using the word "Easter." - Acts 12:4 The Hebrew term PESAK was transliterated (not translated) into the Greek script 29 times as PASCHA. The KJV's use of the word Easter at Acts 12:4 defies logic, since if it could be justified in one instance, then why not all 29 instances? The dirty little secret is that this Catholic tradition overwhelmed the translators, and now everyone is claiming the meaning behind the word Easter is still clean. They are trying to put a new crust over it with claims that it means "dawn" (still based another pagan deity of the dawn, Aurora). Magicians use misdirection to deceive, and Jesuits use casuistry in the same way.

I predicted that when the Truth of the term "Easter" was made known across the world, that it would awaken millions from their slumber. Now it's beginning to happen, and Christian pastors are posting their explanations as fast as they can to reduce the damage to their authority. The Easter Harlot has had a major wardrobe malfunction and the world is going to get a good look at it. Proper nouns aren't translated; the sound remains.

As usual, they are playing on the ignorance of their followers, using "translation" as the universal equivocation device.

They are turning to meanings based on Anglo-Saxon, German, Greek, and Latin. Ishtar, Eastre, Ostern, and many others have no connection with Yahusha's language or His resurrection, but they do relate to Aurora, Aphrodite, Diana, Libertas, Ashtaroth, Durga, and other terms for the mother goddess worshipped by witches. Other wardrobe malfunctions are to come.

The worship of the **host of heaven** by means of Babel's zodiac, or vows to the queen of heaven though every birthday cake, are being shown to have nothing to do with Yahusha's behavior. Yahusha is cleansing the filth from His bride in a worldwide behavior revolution aimed at bearing good fruit.

Here is a recent posting that basically says, *"Move along, there's nothing to see here."* Constantine (the father of Christianity) becomes part of their explanation:

Easter question posted at Jesus.org:

Is Easter Named for a Pagan Goddess?

"Our English word Passover, happily, in sound and sense, almost corresponds to the Hebrew [pesach], of which is a translation (Exodus 12:27). The Greek pascha, formed from the Hebrew, is the name of the Jewish festival, applied invariably in the primitive church to designate the festival of the Lord's resurrection, which took place at the time of the passover.

Our word Easter is of Saxon origin, and of precisely the same import with its German cognate Ostern. The latter is derived from the old Teutonic form of **auferstehn**, Auferstehung, which means "resurrection." The name Easter is undoubtedly preferable to Pascha or Passover, but the latter was the primitive name."

"The word Easter is of Saxon origin, the name is eastre, the goddess of spring in whose honor sacrifices were offered about Passover time each year. By the eighth century Anglo-Saxons had adopted the name to designate the celebration of Christ's resurrection." - from An Ecclesiastical History to the Twentieth Year of the Reign of Constantine, 4th ed., trans. Christian F. Cruse (London: Oxford Univ. Press, 1847).

DID THE EXPLANATION BY JESUS.ORG WORK FOR YOU?
Equivocation is employed to defend the error.
The misdirection is in their translation of the German word, **auferstehn**, which doesn't mean resurrection. It is a word that refers to springtime, and means "to resuscitate."
It's time to wake up now, and be restored to favor with Yahuah.

www.fossilizedcustoms.com/casuistry.html
www.fossilizedcustoms.com/birthday.html
www.fossilizedcustoms.com/easter.html

TORAH INSTITUTE

WHO IS EASTER?

SHE IS GAIA, ASTAROTH, ISHTAR
ARTEMIS, VENUS, APHRODITE
SEMIRAMIS, NATURE, GREAT MOTHER
FRIGGA, LIBERTAS, EOSTRE, DURGA
HATHOR, QUEEN OF HEAVEN

We don't wake up one day doing all these odd things together
because they are derived from anything truthful or beneficial,
but because we are directed to do them by religious and social
pressures. We want to fit in and conform, so we imitate.
When we are shown the Truth, at first it sounds ridiculous.
The next stage is to violently oppose it.
Finally, it is accepted as self-evident.
**"Arise, shine, for your light has come! And the esteem of
Yahuah has risen upon you."** – YashaYahu / Is. 60:1
PLEASE STOP THE ZOMBIE NONSENSE AND WAKE UP

THE DAY THEY WIPED-OUT A COMMANDMENT

"Judaizers" were, and are, those who defy men's teachings, and
observe the Shabath as the day of rest from work. This rest is
emphasized at Hebrews 4, associated with imitating Yahuah,
Who also rested from His work on the 7th day of the week, which
He established as the sign of the Eternal Covenant (Ez 20:12, Ex
31:13, YashaYahu 56:2-7).
**The Catholic council at Laodicea around 364-365 CE states:
"Christians should not Judaize and should not be idle on
the Sabbath, but should work on that day; they should,
however, particularly reverence the Lord's day and, if
possible, not work on it, because they were Christians."**
Huh? They *outlawed* the 4th Commandment?

CATHOLIC NUN   BUDDHIST NUN

Repent, for the reign of Yahuah draws near.
Other books by this author at torahzone.net

Study Scripture in its original Hebrew context
Google: Besorah of Yahusha Natsarim Version
torahzone.net READ REVIEWS AT AMAZON.COM Call 502-261-9833

Renew your mind with the Covenant on the next page.

POB 436044 - LOUISVILLE KY 40253

TORAH OF 𐤉𐤄𐤅𐤄
COVENANT OF KINDNESS
TEACHING HOW TO LOVE

1. I AM YAHUAH YOUR ALAHIM
   HAVE NO OTHER BEFORE MY FACE

2. YOU DO NOT BOW TO IMAGES

3. YOU DO NOT CAST THE NAME OF
   YAHUAH YOUR ALAHIM TO RUIN

4. REMEMBER SHABATH
   TO KEEP IT QODESH

5. RESPECT YOUR FATHER
   AND YOUR MOTHER

6. YOU DO NOT MURDER

7. YOU DO NOT BREAK WEDLOCK

8. YOU DO NOT STEAL

9. YOU DO NOT BEAR FALSE
   WITNESS AGAINST YOUR NEIGHBOR

10. YOU DO NOT COVET YOUR
    NEIGHBOR'S WIFE, HOUSE, FIELD,
    SERVANTS, ANIMALS, OR ANYTHING
    BELONGING TO YOUR NEIGHBOR

LOVE ONE ANOTHER
AS I HAVE LOVED YOU
LOVE YAHUAH, LOVE YOUR NEIGHBOR